W. H. AUDEN
───────

For the Time Being

W. H. AUDEN: CRITICAL EDITIONS

GENERAL EDITOR

Edward Mendelson

Lectures on Shakespeare
Reconstructed and edited by Arthur Kirsch

Juvenilia: Poems, 1922–1928
Expanded Paperback Edition
Edited by Katherine Bucknell

The Sea and the Mirror
A Commentary on Shakespeare's The Tempest
Edited by Arthur Kirsch

The Age of Anxiety
A Baroque Eclogue
Edited by Alan Jacobs

For the Time Being
A Christmas Oratorio
Edited by Alan Jacobs

W. H. AUDEN

For the
Time Being

*   *   *

A Christmas Oratorio

EDITED BY
Alan Jacobs

PRINCETON UNIVERSITY PRESS
PRINCETON AND OXFORD

Published by Princeton University Press, 41 William Street,
Princeton, New Jersey 08540
In the United Kingdom: Princeton University Press, 6 Oxford Street,
Woodstock, Oxfordshire OX20 1TW

press.princeton.edu
Jacket photograph: British-born author and poet W. H. Auden speaking. January
1940. Photo by Hermann/Time & Life Pictures. Courtesy of Getty Images

Library of Congress Cataloging-in-Publication Data
Auden, W. H. (Wystan Hugh), 1907–1973.
For the time being : a Christmas oratorio / W.H. Auden ; edited by Alan Jacobs.
p. cm. — (W. H. Auden: critical editions)
Includes bibliographical references.
ISBN 978-0-691-15827-3 (hardcover : alk. paper)
I. Jacobs, Alan, 1958– II. Title.
PR6001.U4F6 2013
821′.912—dc23
2012036662

British Library Cataloging-in-Publication Data is available

This book has been composed in ITC New Baskerville

Printed on acid-free paper. ∞

Printed in the United States of America

5 7 9 10 8 6 4

CONTENTS

PREFACE

In August of 1941, Constance Rosalie Bicknell Auden died in her sleep at her home in Birmingham, England, at the age of seventy-two. At the time her son W. H. Auden was living in the United States and visiting a friend in Rhode Island. The telephone call announcing her death was taken not by Auden himself but by his companion, Chester Kallman, who then came to Auden's bedroom and gave him the welcome news that they would not be attending a party that evening that Auden had been dreading. Then Kallman told him why they would be staying home.

Auden was stunned and grieved, and not only because he had been very close to his mother all his life. He was already in a state of emotional fragility, having learned just the month before that Kallman, whom he loved and to whom he considered himself married, had been having sex with other men and meant to continue the practice. Auden would later write, "When mother dies, one is, for the first time, really alone in the world and that is hard"; but that experience of isolation was surely made far more intense through its arriving in the midst of hopes already ruined. Some months after the crisis he told his friend James Stern, "I never really loved anyone before, and then when he got through the wall, he became so much a part of my life that I keep forgetting that he is a separate person, and having discovered love, I have also discovered what I never knew before, the dread of being abandoned and left alone."

These experiences were made still more complex for Auden by his recent return to the Christian faith in which he had been raised. His mother's attachment to High Church Anglicanism had shaped his early religious experience, and it was that form of Christian belief and practice that Auden had embraced in the year or so preceding her death. In poems he wrote during this period, especially "In Sickness and in Health," Auden clearly associated his transition from unbelief to belief with his transition from a sexual promiscuity focused on physical beauty to faithful marital love. The wedding ring he began to wear at some point in 1939—"this round O of faithfulness we swear"— testified simultaneously to his love for Kallman and to his belief in the God whom in another poem he called "the author and giver of all good things."

In a Christmas verse letter to Kallman he wrote, "Because it is through you that God has chosen to show me my beatitude, / As this morning I think of the Godhead I think of you." It is noteworthy that this letter was written in the Christmas season of 1941, *after* the revelation of Chester's infidelity. Rather than allow the complex, mutually reinforcing interrelations among his love of his mother, his love of Chester, and his embrace of Christianity to unravel, Auden made the decision to renew and reinvigorate them, by an act of intellectual and poetic will. The chief public evidence of this decision is "For the Time Being: A Christmas Oratorio," which he began writing about two months after his mother's death. It would become the most explicitly Christian and biblical poem of his career; it includes a character based on himself—Joseph, the husband of Mary; and it is dedicated to the memory of Constance Rosalie Auden.

In preparing this edition I have been the beneficiary of much direct and indirect assistance. My most abundant thanks must go to Edward Mendelson, who, as he did when I was working on *The Age of Anxiety*, offered counsel, instruction, and photocopies of obscure documents. Among the other Auden scholars who have gone before me, my greatest debts are to John Fuller, Nicholas Jenkins, and Arthur Kirsch: they have laid the foundation for the annotations and explanations presented here. The staffs of the Manuscripts Division of the Princeton University Library, the Harvard University Archives, and especially the

Berg Collection at the New York Public Library have been cordial, helpful, and endlessly patient. The staff of Princeton University Press have been, as always, absolute paragons of professional competence in all matters editorial. I owe a special debt to Lauren Lepow for her sharp eye and acute editorial intelligence. The endowers of the Clyde S. Kilby Chair of English at Wheaton College have generously supported my scholarship by enabling me to visit the aforementioned institutions when necessary. As when I was working on *The Age of Anxiety*, Aubrey Buster assisted cheerfully and skillfully.

INTRODUCTION

THE POEM

Auden's arrival in America in January of 1939 inaugurated an era of remarkable productivity for him that would last throughout the Second World War. To some extent this was economically necessary: he had to write critical prose to make a living. But Auden was also in the process of reassessing his whole intellectual and poetic equipment, and this required an enormous amount of reading and, then, writing about what he read. The dozens of reviews that he produced during the war years are, taken collectively, the work of a man thinking through the largest of issues in the most thoroughgoing of ways. Auden wrote about politics, philosophy, psychoanalysis, art, erotic love, and marriage; and he wrote about most of these topics in theologically inflected language.

In his first two years in America he also produced many short poems and completed two major artistic projects. One was the libretto for *Paul Bunyan,* an operetta whose music was composed by Auden's friend Benjamin Britten. The second project was a long verse epistle, "New Year Letter," in which he strove to work through his recent reading and thinking, especially about art, politics, and human community. The poem explores theology only in its final lines and only by implication: when Auden wrote it, he had not yet committed himself to Christianity.

Auden and Britten had worked together in England on several projects, starting with the remarkable short film *Night Mail* (1936), a product of the General Post Office Film Unit. They had also collaborated on work for the Group Theatre in London, as Britten set texts Auden had written in collaboration with Christopher Isherwood. Britten and his partner Peter Pears—a singer for whom Britten composed much music over the years—had come to New York soon after Auden, and for a time they all lived in the same house in Brooklyn Heights, so it was natural for them to continue their collaboration.

Paul Bunyan did not succeed, either artistically or commercially: it was first performed in 1941, more than a year after it was completed, and then only by a student group at Columbia University. Britten and Auden alike were working in idioms not fully natural to them, and Auden's attempt in his libretto to write a distinctively American English never wholly convinces and at times induces cringing. Yet he enjoyed working with Britten; moreover, the world of classical vocal music— especially high opera, to which Kallman had introduced him—had become a source of increasing fascination. It made sense, then, that when he considered another major artistic project, it would be a words-and-music work, but one that arose more directly from the ideas and concerns that were driving his self-transformation—and that had recently led him from the speculative meditations of "New Year Letter" to explicit religious commitment.

A few weeks after his mother's death Auden moved to Ann Arbor to begin a year of teaching at the University of Michigan. By October Auden was drafting an application for a Guggenheim Fellowship in which he proposed to write "a long poem in several parts about Christmas, suitable for becoming the basis of a text for a large-scale musical oratorio." (Asked to identify the project's significance, he simply wrote, "There may still be much to be discovered about ways of combining language and music.") If an operetta about Paul Bunyan written by two Englishmen had been a peculiar enterprise, a poem about Christmas might be thought even less promising: rescuing the validly sayable from a morass of sentimental associations and purely secular observances would be a difficult task indeed.

Yet Auden had come to believe that all the matters he was strenuously reassessing—art, community, erotic love, politics, psychology—

had been fundamentally altered by a single event: the entry of God into human history, what Christians call the Incarnation. The Christ child, as every character agrees in the poem he would write, changes everything. And that radical disruption of the world, and therefore of all the things human beings typically think about the world, needed to be accounted for. Auden set about that task.

Auden had always read widely, but late in 1939 he wrote to a friend, "I have never written nor read so much. For the first time I am leading a life which remotely approximates to the way I think I ought to live." Much of this reading was theological, including his literary reading: he studied Blake and Dostoevsky for their theological insights, along with Augustine, Pascal, Kierkegaard, and many others. These inquiries would deeply inform "For the Time Being."

Two themes dominated Auden's theological reflections during the war years. The first was essentially private and personal: a recognition of what Martin Luther called "the bondage of the will," the sinner's simple helplessness to do what is right. As St. Paul puts it, in tortured syntax, "In me (that is, in my flesh) dwelleth no good thing: for to will is present with me; but how to perform that which is good I find not. For the good that I would I do not: but the evil which I would not, that I do" (Romans 7:18–19). It was Kierkegaard who, in his characteristically paradoxical way, convinced Auden that this lamentable condition paves the way for the greatest of blessings, forgiveness—thus the title of the sermon that concludes *Either/Or*: "The Edifying in the Thought that Against God We Are Always in the Wrong." This vision of sinners under universal judgment and wholly dependent on the mercy of God deeply appealed to Auden, and it turns up repeatedly in his poems in his first American years: "All will be judged," he writes in "At the Grave of Henry James"; "Beloved, we are always in the wrong," he writes in "In Sickness and in Health." For some years the Kierkegaardian form of this Pauline insight provided the first principle of Auden's theology, though eventually he would come to see the perils of overemphasizing it.

Auden's second chief theological theme during this period looked
not at the inner life but at the public sphere, though it too centered
on a paradox. An itinerant prophet named Jesus claimed to be the Mes-
siah of Israel, but though he was not accepted as such by most Jews,
the religion that centered on him became, within three hundred years,
the official religion of the Roman Empire. Surely little could be stranger
than an intersection of Jewish messianic expectation and *Romanitas*;
yet that intersection became arguably the central event in the history
of the Western world. The two books that primarily guided Auden in
his attempts to come to terms with this event were *The Descent of the
Dove* by Charles Williams (1939) and Charles Norris Cochrane's *Chris-
tianity and Classical Culture* (1940).

In 1956 Auden wrote, "I have been reading and rereading *The De-
scent of the Dove* for some sixteen years now and I find it a source of
intellectual delight and spiritual nourishment which remains inex-
haustible." (Williams himself, an editor with Oxford University Press
in London whom Auden had first met while working on *The Oxford
Book of Light Verse*, had a similarly powerful effect on him. He would
write of their initial meeting, "For the first time in my life, I felt myself
in the presence of personal sanctity.") Writing in 1956 Auden would
single out for commendation Williams's "orthodoxy of ... imagina-
tion" and his "ecumenical passion"—"Never was there a historian more
courteous to all alike"—but when he first read the book, he seems to
have been struck primarily by its political theology, its reading of the
whole of history as complicit in a narrative of redemption. Williams
gave *The Descent of the Dove* the subtitle *A Short History of the Holy Spirit
in the Church*, and he conceives of history largely in terms of the move-
ments of that Spirit through individual persons and through human
institutions. He begins his book by invoking the upward movement of
Christ's Ascension (Acts 1) and the subsequent downward movement
of the Holy Spirit on the gathered disciples in Jerusalem (Acts 2), and
throughout much of the rest of the book he emphasizes what he calls
"co-inherence," the mutuality of Christian existence: "dying each oth-

er's life, living each other's death," as he puts it in one of his Arthurian poems. Williams's history is therefore dominated by a series of vertical transactions that give rise to a vast and complex network of horizontal ones. And all of those transactions are generated by the energies of divine Love.

The political consequences of this way of reading history are immense. Williams declares that "'The conversion of time by the Holy Ghost' is the title of the grand activity of the Church," and goes on to say that this conversion happens in public space, in a kind of tense negotiation between the Kingdom and the City. Jesus proclaimed the arrival of the Kingdom of God, or Kingdom of Heaven, in our midst; and the conclusion of the last book of the Bible, the Revelation to John, offers a vision of a Heavenly City, the New Jerusalem, as the proper home of humanity. But all this is articulated under Roman rule, in a world dominated by *that* city, thus creating profound tensions between what Augustine would later call the City of God and the City of Man. Williams puts the problem in his usual paradoxical, teasing way: "The Kingdom—or, apocalyptically, the City—is the state into which Christendom is called; but, except in vision, she is not yet the City. The City is the state which the Church is to become."

In Williams's analysis, the conversion of the empire under Constantine inaugurates an era in which the relations between the Heavenly and Earthly cities are negotiated with some flexibility and charity; it is only much later, toward the end of the medieval period, the Church comes to strive for "a dominant culture, an achieved society"—that is, a society which believes that it already and now enters into its full inheritance, and therefore is justified in creating what Williams calls "the method of the imposition of belief." But this is destructive of the realization of the Kingdom of Heaven among living persons: "the practice of the Co-inherence seems to drive back more and more secretly into the hearts of the saints, who are few in any age."

This "imposition" produces, as an inevitable reaction, the Reformation, and the hope for a whole Christendom grows dimmer and dimmer; only a few thinkers seem to have a clear vision of how it might be rescued, chief among them, Williams argues, Søren Kierkegaard (then a little-known figure in the English-speaking world). Though Williams covers the post-Reformation period far less thoroughly than he does earlier eras of Christendom, he gives Kierkegaard more attention than anyone except Augustine. This emphasis clearly caught Auden's attention, since he began reading Kierkegaard's *Journals* at about this time, in an Oxford University Press edition whose production had been overseen by Williams. Kierkegaard's insistence on the inevitably paradoxical character of the Christian message, especially in the modern age, and on the centrality of suffering to the Christian life, indicates for Williams the possible routes by which "the Order of the Co-inherence" might be restored—and with it, eventually, Christendom itself.

Auden read *The Descent of the Dove* in early 1940; it is likely that he encountered Cochrane's *Christianity and Classical Culture* a few months later. As writers and as personalities, Williams and Cochrane could scarcely be more different: Williams is eccentric, paradoxical, and mystical, while Cochrane is scholarly, assured, and urbane. Williams is a largely self-educated Cockney who somehow drifted into a job in publishing, Cochrane an Oxford-educated academic. Both men's books are urgent and charged with energy, but where Williams's energy gathers in his language, Cochrane's arises purely from ideas. The rhyming of their arguments struck Auden forcibly.

In 1944 Auden convinced the *New Republic* to allow him to review Cochrane's book. He begins the review by stating that in the four years since the book's appearance he has read it "many times," and has become increasingly convinced of its importance to an understanding not just of the ancient world but also of the contemporary one. Cochrane's revolutionary insight, Auden argues, lies in his claim that the Roman state is best understood as an inadequate answer to a philosophical problem, the problem of how to give meaning and value to human life. As Cochrane announces at the outset of his book,

the Roman state is based on certain core premises of classical philoso-
phy that yield the belief "that it was possible to attain a goal of perma-
nent security, peace and freedom through political action.... This no-
tion the Christians denounced with uniform vigor and consistency."
He asserts that "the fall of Rome was the fall of an idea, or rather of a
system of life based upon a complex of ideas which may be described
broadly as those of Classicism; and the deficiencies of Classicism ...
were destined sooner or later to involve the system in ruin." The suc-
cess of Christianity in the empire was largely due to its ability to refute
the absolute claims of *Romanitas* and to demonstrate that (in Auden's
words) "the Christian faith can make sense of man's private and social
experience, and classical philosophy cannot."

So in Cochrane's account the error of Rome was to presume a *politi-
cal* response to a *philosophical* problem; the Christian Gospel gave a
more adequate answer, one that redefined the place of the political.
Rome said that the human world can be saved "through submission to
the 'virtue and fortune' of a political leader" who is a human repre-
sentation of divine power, law, and necessity; Christianity responds
with a story of a God who, acting voluntarily according to love, sacri-
fices himself for his creatures and thereby inaugurates a new order, a
new City, grounded in the human imitation of that love. In this radical
reconstitution of *Romanitas*, says Auden, "there can, for the Christian,
be no distinction between the personal and the political, for all his re-
lationships are both; every marriage is a *polis*, every *imperium* a family;
and he has to learn to forgive and sacrifice himself for his enemies, as
for his wife and children."

In other words, the Christian must participate in what Williams calls
"the Order of Co-inherence"; to do so is to redefine what it means for
an individual human to flourish—Cochrane refers to early Christian
philosophy as "the discovery of personality"—and simultaneously to re-
define the political order. This redefinition Cochrane describes largely
in social, political, and philosophical terms, while Williams prefers a
mystical language, in keeping with his emphasis on the paradoxical

character of sinful human beings silently directed by the Holy Spirit of God; but in Auden's mind they are both talking about the same world-transforming events.

Moreover, Auden understood both writers to be thinking historically in ways peculiarly relevant to their own moment in time. Williams and Cochrane alike hint at the contemporary application of their arguments, but Auden makes such application quite explicit in his review of *Christianity and Classical Culture*.

> Our period is not so unlike the age of Augustine: the planned society, caesarism of thugs or bureaucracies, paideia, scientia, religious persecution, are all with us. Nor is there even lacking the possibility of a new Constantinism; letters have already begun to appear in the press, recommending religious instruction in schools as a cure for juvenile delinquency; Mr. Cochrane's terrifying description of the "Christian" empire under Theodosius should discourage such hopes of using Christianity as a spiritual benzedrine for the earthly city.

Auden might also have been thinking here of Williams's lament for the spiritual consequences of "the method of the imposition of belief." Auden's recognition that those last few centuries of the Roman Empire might serve as a mirror for the twentieth-century self-immolation of the West is the initiating insight of the project that would become "For the Time Being."

It seems, then, that Auden had determined to produce a large work that would in some fashion pay tribute to his mother and to the Christianity that they shared when he was young and had come to share again in the last year of her life; that would in some fashion address the public crisis of the West that had led to the Second World War; that would in some fashion address the very personal crisis that had come to him as a result of Kallman's infidelity. Up to this point in his career when Auden had embarked on large-scale projects, he had tended to cast them in dramatic form and to work with collaborators. He would follow that practice now. Quite early on he settled on the oratorio as the proper form, the Nativity narrative from the Gospels (primarily Luke) as the source text, and Britten as the composer. He began to write.

According to the Christian liturgical calendar each year begins with the season of Advent, which uniquely concerns itself with past and future events: it remembers the first coming ("advent") of the Messiah and looks forward to the day when, as the Nicene Creed puts it, Christ "will come again in glory to judge the living and the dead." To be a Christian is to live between these two advents, to be thankful for the salvation brought by the first Advent and to be soberly penitent in light of Christ's inevitable return in judgment. The believer therefore lives poised, as it were, on a cusp, with Before and After falling off on either side of the moment.

This is a major theme of another book that for a time influenced Auden deeply, Paul Tillich's *The Interpretation of History* (1936). That work became famous for its treatment of the biblical term *kairos*, "the fullness of time" or "the appointed time," which is opposed to *kronos* (sequential or "clock" time) and—more important for Tillich—*logos*, the timeless eternal Word. Tillich seeks to describe time not as "mere duration," "but rather qualitatively fulfilled time, the moment that is creation and fate. We call this fulfilled moment, the moment of time approaching us as fate and decision, *kairos*." It comes to us as fate because we have no power to alter or delay its arrival; it comes to us as decision because we *must* respond in some way to it. This condition is largely what Auden means by "the time being": to be faced with the necessity of radical choice, but a choice that must be made as a kind of leap of faith, since the fateful moment does not impose an interpretation but rather calls one forth from us. This was true even for those who saw Jesus in the flesh, but still more true for those who encounter the Christian claims in this in-between time. A response is invited, even in a sense demanded, but what that response will be is neither enforced nor predetermined.

The Nativity narrative is particularly fertile ground for a poetic embodiment of these reflections because in it the Incarnate Word is present but silent. The Christ child does not speak or act, but is rather the object of speech and action. This stage of the Incarnation is congenial also to Auden's views about the representation of the sacred, which were consistently skeptical and dubious. As he would later write,

> The Incarnation, the coming of Christ in the form of a servant who cannot be recognized by the eye of flesh and blood, but only by the eye of faith, puts an end to all claims of the imagination to be the faculty which decides what is truly sacred and what is profane. A pagan god can appear on earth in disguise but, so long as he wears his disguise, no man is expected to recognize him nor can. But Christ appears looking just like any other man, yet claims that He is the Way, the Truth and the Life, and that no man can come to God the Father except through Him. The contradiction between the profane appearance and the sacred assertion is impassible to the imagination.

It makes perfect sense for a reader of Tillich who has these suspicions to write a thoroughly Christian poem in which Christ does not, in the strict sense, appear at all.

In light of all these reflections, it cannot be surprising that the poem's mood at its outset is not festive but rather anxious, full of foreboding: dominated, then, by the prospect of the second rather than the first Advent. Thus the clear indications early in the poem of a contemporary setting: the second line of the opening section mentions "the clock on the mantelpiece," the fourth refers to a mirror. (Clocks and mirrors are not only modern instruments, but also central images for the whole poem.) In the second section of Part 1 the mirror appears again, this time set "over the fireplace" of a house with a living room and a wine cellar. Moreover, "The violent howling of winter and war has become / Like a juke-box tune that we dare not stop."

The furnishings of the modern world recur throughout this poem, even when it commences its retelling of the Gospel narrative, and when Auden sent this poem to his father, the older man—a learned and cultured physician, but not a litterateur—expressed some perplexity about this. Auden wrote him a long letter explaining his method:

> Sorry you are puzzled by the oratorio. Perhaps you were expecting a purely historical account as one might give of the battle of Waterloo, whereas I was trying to treat it as a religious event which eternally recurs every time it is accepted. Thus the historical fact that the shepherds were *shepherds* is religiously accidental—the religious fact is that they were the poor and humble of this world for whom at this moment the historical expression is the city-proletariat, and so on with all the other figures. What we know of Herod, for instance, is that he was a Hellenised-Jew and a political ruler. Accordingly I have made him express the intellectual's eternal objection to Christianity—that it replaces objectivity with subjectivity—and the politician's eternal objection that it regards the state as having only a negative role. (See Marcus Aurelius.) ...
>
> I am not the first to treat the Christian data in this way, until the 18th Cent. it was always done, in the Mystery Plays for instance or any Italian paintings. It is only in the last two centuries that religion has been "humanized," and therefore treated historically as something that happened a long time ago, hence the nursery picture of Jesus in a nightgown and a Parsifal beard.
>
> If a return to the older method now seems startling it is partly because of the acceleration in the rate of historical change due to industrialization—there is a far greater difference between the accidents of life in 1600 AD and in 1942 than between those of 30 AD and 1600.

For Auden, the "humanizing" of religion is effectively the historicizing of it, the construction of a wall to demarcate historical eras. Auden's "return to the older method" is meant to dismantle the historicizing wall and thereby to place the reader within a story that *began* "a long time ago" but *continues*, effectually, today.

But the sense of foreboding that dominates "Advent" reflects the position of a person, or of a whole world, not yet initiated into that history. The second section ends with a flat affirmation—"This is the Abomination. This is the wrath of God"—and the remaining sections of "Advent" are therefore appropriately dotted with questions about this predicament: "Where is that Law for which we broke our own?" "O where is that immortal and nameless Centre from which our points of / Definition and death are all equi-distant?" "How can his knowledge protect his desire for truth from illusion?"

For Auden, a certain kind of temperament provides exceptionally fertile ground for the cultivation of illusion: the "Arcadian," he would come to call it, the celebrant of an ideally innocent past—or, in the terms of this poem, the one who longs to return to the Garden. What was once the Garden has become "our dreadful wood": an evocation of the *selva oscura* in which Dante the pilgrim found himself lost in the first lines of his Comedy. In a fundamental sense, Auden says, "the garden is the only place there is"—it is the proper home of humanity— but it cannot simply be reclaimed: after all, angels with flaming swords have been posted to prevent reentry (Genesis 3:24). Humanity must turn its back on that original Garden and look for the experience of wholeness elsewhere; "but you will not find it / Until you have looked for it everywhere and found nowhere that is not a desert." Arcadianism is, in brief, the refusal of this hard and purgative path, and the corresponding longing for the angels and their swords simply to go away. Hoping to return to the Garden is like hoping to return to the womb.

Auden knew this temptation well—his own temperament was resolutely Arcadian—and for that reason he mocked it ruthlessly. In the poem that would follow "For the Time Being," "The Sea and the Mir-

ror," he did this through the character of Caliban, who ventriloquizes
the Arcadian plea:

> Carry me back, Master, to the cathedral town where the canons
> run through the water meadows with butterfly nets and the old
> women keep sweetshops in the cobbled side streets.... Give me
> my passage home, let me see that harbour once again just as it
> was before I learned the bad words.... Look, Uncle, look. They
> have broken my glasses and I have lost my silver whistle. Pick me
> up, Uncle, let little Johnny ride away on your massive shoulders
> to recover his green kingdom ...

In "For the Time Being" his spokesmen are more gentle, simply point-
ing fallen, broken people toward the necessary desert, a wilderness
like the one that separated the Israelites from their Promised Land.
The biblical narrative, onto which he has chosen to map the structure
of his poem, is one that moves relentlessly forward: from the Garden
to the Flood, from the Flood to the call of Abraham, from Abraham
to the call of Moses, and so on until the Advent of the Messiah, it is
a linear progression. And to those in the middle of the story, those
caught in "the time being," the general outlines of the narrative can
be nearly impossible to discern.

What is called for, then, is an acceptance of absurdity and incom-
prehension: "Therefore, see without looking, hear without listening,
breathe without asking." In advocating this quietness of spirit Auden
assumes an Eastern tone otherwise uncommon with him, and this is
largely an effect of Auden's deep admiration, at this moment in his
career, of T. S. Eliot. Auden always admired Eliot personally—he once
told Louise Bogan, "I shall never be as great and good a man if I live
to be a hundred"—but his opinion of Eliot's poetry fluctuated and
was rarely very high. During the Second World War it was at its peak.
In 1943 Auden concluded a lecture at Swarthmore by reading the
concluding lines of the recently published "Little Gidding" and then
naming Eliot "the greatest poet now living, ... one whose personal and

professional example are to every other and lesser writer at once an inspiration and a reproach."

As the notes at the end of this volume will show, Eliot is often echoed in "For the Time Being," but Auden also knew that Eliot often succumbed to the temptation of Arcadianism; and every homage to Eliot, and Eliot's seeking for the impassive nonattachment so central to Hinduism and Buddhism, is accompanied also by a critique. That critique begins in the next part of the poem.

Because a straightforward return to the Garden is impossible, answers to the challenging questions pressed at the end of "Advent" must be sought elsewhere. Possibilities come into view in "The Annunciation," which somewhat surprisingly begins neither with Mary nor with the angel Gabriel but with the "Four Faculties" as described by Carl Jung in his book *Psychological Types*: Thought, Intuition, Sensation, and Feeling. Auden was a born taxonomist who loved making charts and fitting people, events, and artworks into them, and at this time he was particularly interested in Jung's categories. (Many years later, though, he would open to this section in a copy of the poem and write in the margin, "Bosh, straight from Jung.") In the notebook containing most of the surviving drafts of the poem, he attempts to relate Jung's four types to other categorical schemes: like the people who would later develop the Meyers-Briggs Type Indicator system, he employs Jung's opposition between the Introvert and the Extravert, and adds some binary pairs of his own: Objectivity/Subjectivity, Active/Passive, Actual/Possible, Ethical/Observational. He even associates the four Faculties with the four humors of early modern medicine, seeing Thought as "Melancholic," Intuition as "Lymphatic" (instead of the usual Phlegmatic), Sensation as "Sanguine," and Feeling as "Choleric."

In the poem these Faculties are made to serve a theological purpose: "We who are four were / Once but one, / Before his act of / Rebellion," which is to say that before the Fall, Adam's intellectual, perceptual, emotional, and sensory capabilities were unified and governed by a single unerring impulse. What Eliot claimed to be true for the Elizabethan dramatists, that "thought and feeling were one," Auden says was true only in Eden. To be sure, we suffer from a "dissociation of sensibility," but that is the condition of *all* the children of Adam. To think that in any particular historical period—whether Eliot's Elizabethan age or Yeats's "Byzantium during the reign of Justinian"—human beings could achieve that oneness of being is pure Arcadian sentimentality. After Adam's "act of / Rebellion" our faculties split, and now struggle with one another for dominance. A kind of *psychomachia* or internal warfare is the common lot of humanity, a point Auden would develop more completely in his later and longer poem *The Age of Anxiety.*

The Faculties peer into the Garden from which Adam and Eve were exiled. That exile initiated time as we know it (thus the clocks) and anxious self-consciousness (thus the mirrors). Auden sets the Annunciation, the archangel Gabriel's telling young Mary that she will be impregnated by the Holy Spirit of God and will bear the world's Savior, in the Garden of Eden to indicate that Mary's acceptance of her role is the key event in the renewal of the world that had been broken by our first parents. Auden here embraces the ancient theological commonplace that Mary's humble obedience in response to Gabriel's invitation—"And Mary said, Behold the handmaid of the Lord; be it unto me according to thy word" (Luke 1:38)—inverts and sets right Eve's prideful response to the serpent's invitation to eat the one fruit that God had forbidden. But in characterizing the fundamental human need addressed by Mary's obedience as a psychic one, the anxiety produced by self-consciousness and inauthentic being, Auden is drawing not on ancient sources but on a theological movement generated primarily by Kierkegaard and developed by his twentieth-century successors, especially Karl Barth, Paul Tillich, Auden's friend Reinhold Niebuhr, and in a sense Jung himself. This dynamic union of contemporaneity and traditionalism characterizes Auden's Christian thought.

Though Luke describes the Annunciation in detail, it is Matthew who gives us the response of Mary's fiancé to her pregnancy: "Then Joseph her husband, being a just man, and not willing to make her a public example, was minded to put her away privily" (1:19); only then does he get angelic instructions laying out *his* part in the story, a part it could not have been easy for him to accept. Of the poem's third section, "The Temptation of St. Joseph," Auden once said, "Joseph is me." After discovering Kallman's infidelity, Auden was tempted to kill Kallman, his lover, or both, once even closing his hands around Kallman's throat while the younger man was sleeping. Kallman's lover was an upper-class English sailor, and in the complete typescripts of the poem—that is, at a very advanced stage in the composition—Auden was including this detail in the poem itself, in this late-deleted stanza of Joseph's account:

> Disjointed items stopped my life to say
> How proud they were to satisfy
>   My own true love:
> Hair, muscle, clothing noses, necks,
> A prince's purse, a sailor's sex
>   Appeal;
> And my horns grew up to the sky;
> When I asked if they were real,
> All giggled and ran away.

The horns are of course those of the cuckolded husband.

Some years later, in an essay identifying the key events in his conversion to Christianity, Auden would describe his psychic condition in those days:

And then, providentially—for the occupational disease of poets is frivolity—I was forced to know in person what it is like to feel oneself the prey of demonic powers, in both the Greek and the

Christian sense, stripped of self-control and self-respect, behaving like a ham actor in a Strindberg play.

It is telling that Auden calls this experience "providential": he was rescued from frivolity by having to confront his own potential murderousness, his own powerlessness when possessed by the demon of jealousy—the extent to which against God he is always in the wrong.

But none of this characterizes the Joseph of his poem. Rather, that figure is befuddled, ignorant of what everyone else seems to know, an object of pity; most important of all, he seems ready to forgive Mary and trust God, if he can manage it:

> All I ask is one
> Important and elegant proof
> That what my Love had done
> Was really at your will
> And that your will is Love.

When this request is denied, Joseph falls silent. Silence can never be definitively interpreted, but throughout the passage there is no indication of anger, only a desperate wish that the trust he is already placing in his betrothed and in God will not be misplaced. And indeed, by the time that he wrote these words Auden had determined to continue his relationship with Kallman, even though Kallman made it clear to him that that relationship would no longer have a sexual dimension. He confessed to James Stern, "I love him to distraction and cant help boring my friends about him," and at Christmas 1941 he wrote a long verse letter to Kallman that includes this hopeful affirmation:

Because, although our love, beginning Hans Andersen, became Grimm, and there are probably even grimmer tests to come, nevertheless I believe that if only we have faith in God and in each other, we shall be permitted to realize all that love is intended to be;

As this morning I think of the Good Friday and the Easter Sunday implicit in Christmas Day, I think of you.

But the poem's Joseph is only partly a self-portrait: in another sense, one that carries more weight in the poem as a whole, he is a representative of his sex. The poem's Narrator—serving, as he often does, to provide corrective or supplemental theological context for us, especially when the characters in the midst of the story don't clearly understand what's happening to them—says, "you must now atone, / Joseph, in silence and alone" for the multiple injuries your fellow males have inflicted on women. Joseph must accept his completely marginal role in the story, as the birth of the Messiah is accomplished by parthenogenesis, without need for his services. Joseph thus becomes, not precisely a "Christ-figure," but a kind of personified adumbration of the vicarious suffering his wife's son will eventually perform for the world.

So the presence of the Four Faculties indicates a narrative of original psychic integration broken to pieces by the Fall, with the Incarnation marking the beginnings of reintegration. But then, in the latter sections of "The Annunciation," Auden begins to apply a similar analysis to the social world. Those who rejoice at Mary's acceptance of her task include "number and weight" (the inanimate world) and, among human beings, the great, the small, the young, and the old. The developing story of redemption is received by all, affects all, but in different ways according not only to psychological inclination but also to social emplacement. This emergence of a social taxonomy marks a key transition in the poem: persons shaped by various combinations of the Four Faculties enter the public realm, and that realm will be consistently present for the rest of the poem. At the end of "The Temptation of St. Joseph" Joseph and Mary—neither of them exceptional in themselves, but only in the roles they have been chosen to play—become the proper patrons of "common ungifted / Natures," of the "romantics" and the "bourgeoisie," people who according to their varying natures follow the "Average Way" but who are nevertheless the objects of God's redemptive love.

The fourth part of the poem, "The Summons," concerns itself with the exceptional, to whom the arrival of this Child comes as worrisome news, or worse: says the Star of the Nativity, "I am that star most dreaded by the wise," who fear "the doom of orthodox sophrosyne." *Sophrosyne* means moderation or temperance ("nothing too much"), and the radical intrusion of God into history threatens to disrupt any and all attempts to employ disciplined, methodical thought to bring the human world under rational control. The natural scientist, the philosopher, and the social scientist alike must confront both their inevitable failure and the vices their attempts at control have led them to.

Something fundamental to Auden's reading of history appears when the purgative journey of these Wise Men is interrupted by a chorus praising Caesar. Cochrane argued that the Roman imperial project justified itself by promising to solve the most intractable problems of classical philosophy and thereby to make the Good Life not only possible but inevitable. In this "fugal-chorus" Auden translates this claim into contemporary terms. When the projects of modern natural science, philosophy, and social science are absorbed by the State—an absorption dramatically accelerated by war—then twentieth-century Caesarism achieves social domination more comprehensive than anything the Romans could have dreamed of. The state that controls the economy ("the Kingdom of Credit Exchange") *and* an ever-expanding pharmaceutical industry ("the Kingdom of Organic Dwarfs") is well-placed to make the final conquest: "the Kingdom of Popular Soul."

Auden repeatedly insisted, throughout the war, on the absolute necessity of defeating Hitler, and indeed sought a meaningful role: after being rejected by the draft board for his homosexuality, he at one point in 1942 considered signing up for the Merchant Marine. (At the war's end he joined the U.S. Strategic Bombing Survey in Germany, receiving as a civilian the equivalent rank of major.) But much of his *writing* during the war, and immediately after, was driven by concern for what sort of Western society would emerge from an Allied victory. Thus his statement, in 1944, about a new translation of *Grimm's Fairy Tales*: "It is unlikely that there will be another event during the current publishing season as important as this," and the peroration of his review:

> So let everyone read these stories till they know them backward and tell them to their children with embellishments—they are not sacred texts—and then, in a few years, the Society for the Scientific Diet, the Association of Positivist Parents, the League for the Promotion of Worthwhile Leisure, the Co-operative Camp of Prudent Progressives and all other bores and scoundrels can go jump in the lake.

This emphasis infuriated Randall Jarrell: a year later in *Partisan Review* he wrote, "In the year 1944 these prudent, progressive, scientific, coöperative 'bores and scoundrels' were the enemies with whom Auden found it necessary to struggle. Were these *your* enemies, reader? They were not mine." Jarrell misunderstands Auden's position: being unable to fight himself, he could do nothing about the progress of the war. But as a poet and thinker he could, and needed to be, concerned about the cultural consequences of even a successful war; like many other intellectuals at this time, including Reinhold Niebuhr, he feared that "the danger is that, in order to win [the war], the democracies will construct an anti-fascist political religion, and so, by becoming like their enemies, lose the peace." This accounts for his decision to write, in wartime, a long poem that has relatively little to say about war but a great deal to say about the dangers of Caesarism, especially in the soft-totalitarian form in which he felt it was likely to emerge in the West.

Thus after the chorus's praise—"Great is Caesar; God must be with Him"—the Narrator provides a voice of gentle dissent. Caesar's conquests are not complete after all: within the Kingdom of Credit Exchange there are "problems" that, "experts" reassure us, are "practically solved"; "public morale" is improving only with "restrictions / Upon aliens and free-thinking Jews"; and then there is the threat posed by "the rising power of the Barbarian in the North." It would appear that the perfected empire is always a promise but never quite a reality. Moreover, the Narrator's affirmation that "Powers and Times are not gods but mortal gifts from God"—an echo of "Render unto Caesar the things which are Caesar's, and unto God the things that are God's"— quietly but completely repudiates the claims made for Caesar's empire in the fugal-chorus. Preceding that chorus the Narrator had asked us to "stand motionless and hear" Caesar's proclamation; now his instruction is simply, "Let us pray." And not to Caesar.

After this imperial interruption, the poem's social taxonomy returns with the introduction of the Shepherds. They are, as Auden explained to his father, "the poor and humble of this world" who, unlike the Wise, do not seek control—but who also refuse to be simplified and objectified, refuse "to behave like a cogwheel / When one knows one is no such thing." Their role is to watch and wait, striving to maintain hope. Thus to them the Chorus of Angels proclaims, though with altered pronouns, the declaration from Isaiah 9: "For unto us a child is born, unto us a son is given."

And now, with the fifth part, "At the Manger," the Child is indeed born, and Mary, the Wise Men, and the Shepherds gather around him. (Joseph has disappeared from our view until the last pages of the poem.) Mary, who understands what her son is called to do and be— in Renaissance paintings of the Annunciation she is sometimes portrayed reading the "suffering servant" passage from Isaiah 53—simply wants her "Little One" to sleep and dream while he may, but Auden uses the responses of the Wise Men and the Shepherds to illustrate what may well have been his favorite binary opposition, that between Arcadians and Utopians. The Arcadian temperament we have already explored, and it is manifested here in the Shepherds, who "never left the place where [they] were born" and are afflicted by the "sullen wish to go back to the womb" and to have "no future." By contrast, the

Utopian temperament looks with "arrogant longing" towards a per-
fected future and therefore wishes "To have no past"; it is embodied
in the Wise Men and, by extension, in all who seek shaping power
over their worlds.

Thus earlier in the poem the Shepherds, in the section "Levers
nudge the aching wrist," hear voices tempting them to suicide; at first
their only reply is "No, I don't know why, / But I'm glad I'm here," but
once they have seen the Child, they cry, "O here and now our endless
journey starts." Only the Child has the power to sweep away "the filth
of habit from [their] hearts." Conversely, the Wise Men, with their
Utopian temperament, must arrest their determination to remake the
world, and instead must find all meaning in the Child: so at the man-
ger they cry, "O here and now our endless journey stops." Each group
must discover genuine hope by achieving release from its habitual
"phantasy." Earlier in the poem a Chorus had asked, "How can [Man's]
knowledge protect his desire for truth from illusion?" The answer is
that knowledge cannot: such illusions are displaced only by "Living
Love," a Love incarnate in this infant.

The next two parts of the poem, "The Meditation of Simeon" and
"The Massacre of the Innocents," introduce no new themes but rather
develop in more detail ideas already present: the challenge this Child
poses to intellectuals in search of knowledge and to political leaders
in search of power. The characters encountered are therefore a theo-
logian and a king.

Auden's Wise Men are secular intellectuals whose encounter with
the Star of the Nativity, and then with the Child himself, opens them
for the first time to the transcendent. Simeon, though, is a serious
believer, and the challenge the Child poses to his intellectual frame-
work is of a wholly different order. In keeping with his commitment to
contemporaneity, Auden strips the biblical Simeon of his Jewishness:
readers will learn nothing from this poem about how the very idea of

an Incarnate God might have struck a man in Jerusalem who "was just and devout, waiting for the consolation of Israel" (Luke 2:25). Instead we hear from one who can discourse learnedly about Time and the Infinite, the Unconditional and the historically conditioned, the relations between Virtue and Necessity, and the ways that a stenographer might or might not resemble Brünnhilde. Moreover, his language is specifically Christian throughout, paraphrasing or commenting on the early creeds and Augustinian theology. The famous words of the biblical Simeon—"Lord, now lettest thou thy servant depart in peace, according to thy word: For mine eyes have seen thy salvation"—do find their echo here: "having seen Him, not in some prophetic vision of what might be, but with the eyes of our own weakness as to what actually is, we are bold to say that we have seen our salvation." But otherwise his language is resolutely modern and enmeshed in the terminology of post-Kierkegaardian philosophical theology. (How Auden thought this meditation could be accompanied by music is not immediately obvious. Certainly he knew that the density of Simeon's exegesis posed difficulties for performance: he told Theodore Spencer, "The chief reason for the choral interjections in Simeon's prose is to give the audience's attention a moment's rest.")

The burden of Simeon's discourse is essentially twofold: he sets out to explain how God could assume human form, and then how that Incarnation can repair the damage Adam and Eve inflicted on themselves and all their descendants. Simeon's initial task is to close off the Arcadian retreat, then to block the Utopian advance: the first six paragraphs outline what in another poem Auden would call "the alternative routes ... by which the human effort to make its own fortune arrives all eager at its abruptly dreadful end." Simeon conceives of intellectual history as a series of impasses. It was necessary that each of those impasses be explored, and then recognized as offering no outlet, before humanity could be ready to confront the truth of God's purpose: "The Word could not be made Flesh until men had reached a state of absolute contradiction between clarity and despair in which they would have no choice but either to accept absolutely or to reject absolutely."

This absoluteness of response is required by the absolute absurdity of the Word's being made Flesh. Were the claim merely a symbolic one, some interpretative negotiation might be possible; "but of this Child it is the case that He is in no sense a symbol": he is, rather, as human and as historical as any of us. King Herod, in the following section, understands the choice he is offered in precisely the way that Simeon does:

> Why can't people be sensible? I don't want to be horrid. Why can't they see that the notion of a finite God is absurd? Because it is. And suppose, just for the sake of argument, that it isn't, that this story is true, that this child is in some inexplicable manner both God and Man, that he grows up, lives, and dies, without committing a single sin? Would that make life any better? On the contrary it would make it far, far worse. For it can only mean this: that once having shown them how, God would expect every man, whatever his fortune, to lead a sinless life in the flesh and on earth. Then indeed would the human race be plunged into madness and despair. And for me personally at this moment it would mean that God had given me the power to destroy Himself.

The difference between Simeon and Herod lies not in understanding but in response: where Simeon replies to the news by joyously affirming, "we are bold to say that we have seen our salvation," Herod replies with blunt opposition: "I refuse to be taken in." With a sigh of deep regret, he orders the slaughter of the Israelite children.

Simeon the theologian may have found it difficult to accept the idea of God Incarnate, but for Herod it is impossible, because acceptance would require him to relinquish his position as the chief local instrument, in Judaea, of *Romanitas* and the Caesarist project. And this he lacks the strength of will to do. In one of his more striking artistic choices, Auden renders Herod's dilemma and decision comically. Herod's speech opens with a parody of the dedicatory preface to Marcus Aurelius's *Meditations*: he thanks, among others, his brother Sandy, "who married a trapeze artist and died of drink—for so refuting the position of the Hedonists." Herod himself is a Stoic whose self-satisfaction depends on his belief that he carries out his bureaucratic duties faithfully—"I've hardly ever taken bribes"—and that he genuinely desires no harm to anyone: "I'm a liberal," he moans. "I want everyone to be happy." This is the little man behind the curtain of the stentorian imperial chorus in praise of Caesar we heard earlier; here is where the Utopian "phantasy" comes crashing ridiculously, but also violently, to earth. Herod is absurd in a rather less dignified sense than the philosophical. And such, Auden implies, is the fate of all who refuse the absolute contradiction that Simeon accepts.

"For the Time Being" is a poem that ends, as well as begins, in medias res. After the extravagant rhetorical set pieces of Simeon and Herod, the poem draws to a close in a welter of disparate voices. Herod's soldiers sing a jaunty chorus, full of campy slang, about a child adopted and reared, rather than killed, by them. Auden introduces Rachel in order to echo Matthew (2:18) who, in describing Herod's massacre, had echoed the prophet Jeremiah (31:15), who had echoed the grief and bitterness the biblical Rachel suffered because of her barrenness (Genesis 30:1). And then the Holy Family flee Israel, only to be tempted and tormented by "Voices of the Desert" who paint phantasmagorical, Bosch-like images. They continue to Egypt, bearing "our new life."

The reasons for this chaos become manifest when the poem returns, via its calm and straightforward Narrator, to the present moment and a local habitation. For while the Star of the Nativity may have proclaimed "the doom of orthodox sophrosyne," we continue to live in "the moderate Aristotelian city / Of darning and the Eight-Fifteen." While the Christmas narrative, especially as seen by Simeon and Herod, presents us with an absolute contradiction that demands an absolute response, "Once again / As in previous years we have seen the actual Vision and failed / To do more than entertain it as an agreeable / Possibility." The poem's inconclusiveness mimics that of its audience. And therefore it must end not with resolution but with an invitation: to follow, seek, and love the one who is the Way, the Truth, and the Life. It is almost the tone of a revival meeting. In the poetic presentation of spiritual things, Auden would never again be so explicit. In 1946 he told Alan Ansen, "It's the only direct treatment of sacred subjects I shall ever attempt."

On 11 November 1941 Auden wrote to Britten that he had sketched out "Advent." Edward Mendelson has deduced that the writing from that point went more or less as follows: Also in November he began the second part, "The Annunciation." He had completed "The Temptation of St. Joseph" by January 1942, along with the first half of "The Summons." In February he wrote the fugal-chorus in praise of Caesar and the chorale ("Our Father, whose creative Will"). In the next month he wrote "The Vision of the Shepherds." It is not clear when he produced Mary's song "At the Manger" or the long prose meditations of Simeon and Herod, but presumably it was over the next few months. Possibly in July he wrote "The Flight into Egypt." The recitative at the end of the section, "Fly Holy Family," was added very late, sometime around May of 1943.

It is clear that throughout the poem's composition he had a musical setting firmly in mind. In all the surviving notebooks and typescripts— the latter coming very late in the process of composition—speeches are introduced not with the characters' names but with vocal identification: "Tenor Solo," "Boys semi-chorus," and so on. Auden always assumed that Britten would set the poem, and occasionally gave him reports on how the writing was progressing: for instance, in November of 1941 he told Britten, "I have stretched out the First Movement of the Oratorio (1. Chorus and semi-Chorus. 2. Narrator. 3. Trio. 4. Narrator. 5. Chorus) and am starting the 2nd Movement which opens with a boys chorus." In January of 1942 he sent Britten "The

Temptation of St. Joseph" and the first half of "The Summons." But he did not at any point invite Britten to comment or offer suggestions, and after these early communications ended up sending the composer a complete text as a fait accompli. Britten was not pleased. As Peter Pears recalled many years later,

> Ben had expected a text for music, but it turned out to be a major opus, quite unsuitable without *vast* cuts for an oratorio libretto. . . .
> I remember the receipt of "For the Time Being" and how Ben was bitterly disappointed with, for instance, the fugue (a few syllables are enough for a fugue)—Wystan wrote 7 stanzas of 10 lines each. . . . And one of the things Ben had learnt from *Paul Bunyan* was that in creating new large-scale musical works it was of the *utmost importance* that the poet and composer should work together from the outset. When a large section of the work arrived, Ben was desperate at how far Wystan had gone ahead without him, and as he was much more confident of himself as a composer now, he abandoned the whole idea.

Moreover, some of Auden's letters in this period angered Britten: he felt that Auden was patronizing about his relationship with Pears, and too strongly critical of his and Pears's decision to return to England. Their friendship would never recover, and Britten ended up setting only two brief pieces from the oratorio: for a 1944 BBC program called *Poet's Christmas*, he wrote music for the chorale "Our Father, Whose creative Will" and for a "Shepherd's Carol" ("O lift your little pinkie") that Auden removed at a very late stage in the poem's composition. So "For the Time Being" ended up as an oratorio in name only. In the published versions of the poem no vocal indications are present, though a sparse scaffolding—distinguishing individual speakers from choruses, naming some speeches as recitatives—remains in place.

In 1956 an American composer, Philip James, set parts of the poem for women's chorus and string quartet under the title *Chorus of Shepherds and Angels*. And another American composer, Marvin David Levy, did what Britten had declined to do: he set the whole poem to music.

His setting was first performed at Carnegie Hall, by the Collegiate Chorale, in December 1959.

In January 1967 Austrian television broadcast a ninety-minute condensation and adaptation of "For the Time Being" titled *Inzwischen* (Meanwhile), with music written by the Austrian composer Paul Kont. A manuscript survives in the Berg Collection of a note Auden wrote for this production. In it he provides a rationale for his artistic approach very similar to the one he had given to his father more than twenty years earlier:

> Anyone who attempts to use [a sacred event] as a theme for a work of art has to do justice both to the historicity of the event and to its contemporary relevance. This is not easy. If, in treating the Christmas story, he writes as a secular historian would, ie, he makes the clothes, the architecture, the dialogue as nearly what they actually were in Palestine during the reign of Augustus as scholarship can bring them, his piece will, for a twentieth-century artist, be simply an archaeological curiosity. [But] if he makes all his properties and imagery contemporary, the story ceases to be one which the audience are required to believe really happened, and becomes an entertaining myth.

Auden's purpose in "For the Time Being" was to steer between these two dangers, to avoid the "archaeological curiosity" as well as the "entertaining myth," and thereby to present the Nativity narrative as nothing less than a *kairos* moment, an opportunity for his readers to see "the time being" as infinitely rich in possibility and infinitely demanding of choice.

THE TEXT

The chief notebook Auden used when drafting "For the Time Being" was eventually given by the poet to his friend, fan, and occasional patron Caroline Newton. It is now in the Berg Collection of the New York Public Library. Two complete typescripts of the poem survive. One was formerly owned by James Stern, a poet and translator who was for many years a close friend of Auden's; its present location is unknown, although a photocopy is in private hands. The second was sent to Benjamin Britten and is held by the Britten-Pears Library in Aldersburgh, Suffolk. The two typescripts are almost identical, but the second features a number of strike-throughs and contains an autograph appendix listing changes and additions. These variants are indicated in the notes, with the exception of the many small changes in punctuation made in the printed version. (Auden was a notoriously uncertain punctuator and relied on professional copyediting assistance in such matters.) There is also, at Princeton University, a typescript of the first two parts of the poem that differs only in minor ways from the complete typescripts but appears to be slightly earlier than them.

"For the Time Being" was published by Random House on 6 September 1944, bound with "The Sea and the Mirror," the long poem that Auden began writing immediately after completing the oratorio. *For the Time Being* is the title Auden gave to the book. A second impression with corrections appeared in October, but the book was out of print less than a year later, largely because both long poems were included in *The Collected Poetry of W. H. Auden* (Random House, 1945).

A British edition was published by Faber & Faber in March 1945, with its text based on the first American printing, not incorporating the corrections to the second impression, and inadvertently omitting these three lines from the Narrator's last speech:

> Without even a hostile audience, and the Soul endure
> A silence that is neither for nor against her faith
> That God's Will be done, that, in spite of her prayers . . .

The British edition of *For the Time Being* was reprinted several times between 1945 and 1966. All further editions of the poem were based on the text of the second Random House printing. In 1968 the poem appeared in the *Collected Longer Poems* (both Random House and Faber), with corrections, and has been included in each edition of the *Collected Poems* edited by Edward Mendelson, starting in 1976. The text here is nearly identical to that prepared by Edward Mendelson for the most recent edition of the *Collected Poems* (2007), with variations indicated in the notes.

FOR THE TIME BEING

A Christmas Oratorio

*What shall we say then? Shall we continue in sin,
that grace may abound? God forbid.*

ROMANS VI

ADVENT

I

CHORUS

Darkness and snow descend;
The clock on the mantelpiece
Has nothing to recommend,
Nor does the face in the glass
Appear nobler than our own
As darkness and snow descend
On all personality.
Huge crowds mumble—"Alas,
Our angers do not increase,
Love is not what she used to be";
Portly Caesar yawns—"I know";
He falls asleep on his throne,
They shuffle off through the snow:
Darkness and snow descend.

SEMI-CHORUS

Can great Hercules keep his
Extraordinary promise
To reinvigorate the Empire?
Utterly lost, he cannot
Even locate his task but
Stands in some decaying orchard
Or the irregular shadow
Of a ruined temple, aware of
Being watched from the horrid mountains
By fanatical eyes yet
Seeing no one at all, only hearing

The silence softly broken
By the poisonous rustle
Of famishing Arachne.

CHORUS

Winter completes an age
With its thorough levelling;
Heaven's tourbillions of rage
Abolish the watchman's tower
And delete the cedar grove.
As winter completes an age,
The eyes huddle like cattle, doubt
Seeps into the pores and power
Ebbs from the heavy signet ring;
The prophet's lantern is out
And gone the boundary stone,
Cold the heart and cold the stove,
Ice condenses on the bone:
Winter completes an age.

SEMI-CHORUS

Outside the civil garden
Of every day of love there
Crouches a wild passion
    To destroy and be destroyed.
O who to boast their power
Have challenged it to charge? Like
Wheat our souls are sifted
    And cast into the void.

CHORUS

The evil and armed draw near;
The weather smells of their hate

And the houses smell of our fear;
Death has opened his white eye
And the black hole calls the thief
As the evil and armed draw near.
Ravens alight on the wall,
Our plans have all gone awry,
The rains will arrive too late,
Our resourceful general
Fell down dead as he drank
And his horses died of grief,
Our navy sailed away and sank;
The evil and armed draw near.

II

NARRATOR

If, on account of the political situation,
There are quite a number of homes without roofs, and men
Lying about in the countryside neither drunk nor asleep,
If all sailings have been cancelled till further notice,
If it's unwise now to say much in letters, and if,
Under the subnormal temperatures prevailing,
The two sexes are at present the weak and the strong,
That is not at all unusual for this time of year.
If that were all we should know how to manage. Flood, fire,
The desiccation of grasslands, restraint of princes,
Piracy on the high seas, physical pain and fiscal grief,
These after all are our familiar tribulations,
And we have been through them all before, many, many times.
As events which belong to the natural world where
The occupation of space is the real and final fact
And time turns round itself in an obedient circle,

They occur again and again but only to pass
Again and again into their formal opposites,
From sword to ploughshare, coffin to cradle, war to work,
So that, taking the bad with the good, the pattern composed
By the ten thousand odd things that can possibly happen
Is permanent in a general average way.

    Till lately we knew of no other, and between us we seemed
To have what it took—the adrenal courage of the tiger,
The chameleon's discretion, the modesty of the doe,
Or the fern's devotion to spatial necessity:
To practise one's peculiar civic virtue was not
So impossible after all; to cut our losses
And bury our dead was really quite easy: That was why
We were always able to say: "We are children of God,
And our Father has never forsaken His people."

    But then we were children: That was a moment ago,
Before an outrageous novelty had been introduced
Into our lives. Why were we never warned? Perhaps we were.
Perhaps that mysterious noise at the back of the brain
We noticed on certain occasions—sitting alone
In the waiting room of the country junction, looking
Up at the toilet window—was not indigestion
But this Horror starting already to scratch Its way in?
Just how, just when It succeeded we shall never know:
We can only say that now It is there and that nothing
We learnt before It was there is now of the slightest use,
For nothing like It has happened before. It's as if
We had left our house for five minutes to mail a letter,
And during that time the living room had changed places
With the room behind the mirror over the fireplace;
It's as if, waking up with a start, we discovered

Ourselves stretched out flat on the floor, watching our shadow
Sleepily stretching itself at the window. I mean
That the world of space where events re-occur is still there,
Only now it's no longer real; the real one is nowhere
Where time never moves and nothing can ever happen:
I mean that although there's a person we know all about
Still bearing our name and loving himself as before,
That person has become a fiction; our true existence
Is decided by no one and has no importance to love.

That is why we despair; that is why we would welcome
The nursery bogey or the winecellar ghost, why even
The violent howling of winter and war has become
Like a juke-box tune that we dare not stop. We are afraid
Of pain but more afraid of silence; for no nightmare
Of hostile objects could be as terrible as this Void.
This is the Abomination. This is the wrath of God.

III

CHORUS

Alone, alone, about a dreadful wood
Of conscious evil runs a lost mankind,
Dreading to find its Father lest it find
The Goodness it has dreaded is not good:
Alone, alone, about our dreadful wood.

Where is that Law for which we broke our own,
Where now that Justice for which Flesh resigned
Her hereditary right to passion, Mind
His will to absolute power? Gone. Gone.
Where is that Law for which we broke our own?

The Pilgrim Way has led to the Abyss.
Was it to meet such grinning evidence
We left our richly odoured ignorance?
Was the triumphant answer to be this?
The Pilgrim Way has led to the Abyss.

We who must die demand a miracle.
How could the Eternal do a temporal act,
The Infinite become a finite fact?
Nothing can save us that is possible:
We who must die demand a miracle.

IV

RECITATIVE

If the muscle can feel repugnance, there is still a false move
                                                    to be made;
If the mind can imagine to-morrow, there is still a defeat
                                                    to remember;
As long as the self can say "I", it is impossible not to rebel;
As long as there is an accidental virtue, there is a necessary vice:
And the garden cannot exist, the miracle cannot occur.

For the garden is the only place there is, but you will not find it
Until you have looked for it everywhere and found nowhere that is
                                                    not a desert;
The miracle is the only thing that happens, but to you it will not
                                                    be apparent,
Until all events have been studied and nothing happens that you
                                                    cannot explain;
And life is the destiny you are bound to refuse until you have
                                                    consented to die.

Therefore, see without looking, hear without listening, breathe
                      without asking:
The Inevitable is what will seem to happen to you purely by chance;
The Real is what will strike you as really absurd;
Unless you are certain you are dreaming, it is certainly a dream
                      of your own;
Unless you exclaim—"There must be some mistake"—you must
                      be mistaken.

V

CHORUS

O where is that immortal and nameless Centre from
                      which our points of
  Definition and death are all equi-distant? Where
The well of our wish to wander, the everlasting fountain
  Of the waters of joy that our sorrow uses for tears?
O where is the garden of Being that is only known in Existence
  As the command to be never there, the sentence by which
Alephs of throbbing fact have been banished into position,
  The clock that dismisses the moment into the turbine of time?

O would I could mourn over Fate like the others, the
                      resolute creatures,
  By seizing my chance to regret. The stone is content
With a formal anger and falls and falls; the plants are indignant
  With one dimension only and can only doubt
Whether light or darkness lies in the worse direction; and the subtler
  Exiles who try every path are satisfied
With proving that none have a goal: why must Man also acknowledge
  It is not enough to bear witness, for even protest is wrong?

Earth is cooled and fire is quenched by his unique excitement,
    All answers expire in the clench of his questioning hand,
His singular emphasis frustrates all possible order:
    Alas, his genius is wholly for envy; alas,
The vegetative sadness of lakes, the locomotive beauty
    Of choleric beasts of prey, are nearer than he
To the dreams that deprive him of sleep, the powers that compel
                                  him to idle,
    To his amorous nymphs and his sanguine athletic gods.

How can his knowledge protect his desire for truth from illusion?
    How can he wait without idols to worship, without
Their overwhelming persuasion that somewhere, over the high hill,
    Under the roots of the oak, in the depths of the sea,
Is a womb or a tomb wherein he may halt to express
                              some attainment?
    How can he hope and not dream that his solitude
Shall disclose a vibrating flame at last and entrust him forever
    With its magic secret of how to extemporise life?

THE ANNUNCIATION

I

THE FOUR FACULTIES

Over the life of Man
We watch and wait,
The Four who manage
His fallen estate:
We who are four were
Once but one,

Before his act of
Rebellion;
We were himself when
His will was free,
His error became our
Chance to be.

Powers of air and fire,
Water and earth,
Into our hands is given
Man from his birth:

INTUITION

As a dwarf in the dark of
His belly I rest;

FEELING

A nymph, I inhabit
The heart in his breast;

SENSATION

A giant, at the gates of
His body I stand;

THOUGHT

His dreaming brain is
My fairyland.

TUTTI

Invisible phantoms,
The forms we assume are
Adapted to each
Individual humour,

Beautiful facts or true
Generalisations,
Test cases in Law or
Market quotations:
As figures and formulae
Chemists have seen us,
Who to true lovers were
Putti of Venus.

Ambiguous causes
Of all temptation,
We lure men either
To death or salvation:
We alone may look over
The wall of that hidden
Garden whose entrance
To him is forbidden;
Must truthfully tell him
What happens inside,
But what it may mean he
Alone must decide.

II

THOUGHT

The garden is unchanged, the silence is unbroken.
Truth has not yet intruded to possess
Its empty morning nor the promised hour
Shaken its lasting May.

INTUITION

The human night,

Whose messengers we are, cannot dispel
Its wanton dreams, and they are all we know.

SENSATION

My senses are still coarse
From late engrossment in a fair. Old tunes
Reiterated, lights with repeated winks,
Were fascinating like a tic and brought
Whole populations running to a plain,
Making its lush alluvial meadows
One boisterous preposter. By the river
A whistling crowd had waited many hours
To see a naked woman swim upstream;
Honours and reckless medicines were served
In booths where interest was lost
As easily as money; at the back,
In a wet vacancy among the ash cans,
A waiter coupled sadly with a crow.

FEELING

I have but now escaped a raging landscape:
There woods were in a tremor from the shouts
Of hunchbacks hunting a hermaphrodite;
A burning village scampered down a lane;
Insects with ladders stormed a virgin's house;
On a green knoll littered with picnics
A mob of horses kicked a gull to death.

INTUITION

Remembrance of the moment before last
Is like a yawning drug. I have observed
The sombre valley of an industry
In dereliction. Conduits, ponds, canals,

Distressed with weeds; engines and furnaces
At rust in rotting sheds; and their strong users
Transformed to spongy heaps of drunken flesh.
Deep among dock and dusty nettle lay
Each ruin of a will; manors of mould
Grew into empires as a westering sun
Left the air chilly; not a sound disturbed
The autumn dusk except a stertorous snore
That over their drowned condition like a sea
Wept without grief.

THOUGHT

My recent company
Was worse than your three visions. Where I was,
The haunting ghosts were figures with no ground,
Areas of wide omission and vast regions
Of passive colour; higher than any squeak,
One note went on for ever; an embarrassed sum
Stuck on the stutter of a decimal,
And points almost coincident already
Approached so slowly they could never meet.
There nothing could be stated or constructed:
To Be was an archaic nuisance.

INTUITION

Look. There is someone in the garden.

FEELING

The garden is unchanged, the silence is unbroken
For she is still walking in her sleep of childhood:
Many before
Have wandered in, like her, then wandered out

Unconscious of their visit and unaltered,
The garden unchanged, the silence unbroken:
None may wake there but One who shall be woken.

THE ANGEL GABRIEL

Wake.

III

GABRIEL

Mary, in a dream of love
Playing as all children play,
For unsuspecting children may
Express in comic make-believe
The wish that later they will know
Is tragic and impossible;
Hear, child, what I am sent to tell:
Love wills your dream to happen, so
Love's will on earth may be, through you,
No longer a pretend but true.

MARY

What dancing joy would whirl
My ignorance away?
Light blazes out of the stone,
The taciturn water
Bursts into music,
And warm wings throb within
The motionless rose:
What sudden rush of Power
Commands me to command?

GABRIEL

When Eve, in love with her own will,
Denied the will of Love and fell,
She turned the flesh Love knew so well
To knowledge of her love until
Both love and knowledge were of sin:
What her negation wounded, may
Your affirmation heal to-day;
Love's will requires your own, that in
The flesh whose love you do not know,
Love's knowledge into flesh may grow.

MARY

My flesh in terror and fire
Rejoices that the Word
Who utters the world out of nothing,
As a pledge of His word to love her
Against her will, and to turn
Her desperate longing to love,
Should ask to wear me,
From now to their wedding day,
For an engagement ring.

GABRIEL

Since Adam, being free to choose,
Chose to imagine he was free
To choose his own necessity,
Lost in his freedom, Man pursues
The shadow of his images:
To-day the Unknown seeks the known;
What I am willed to ask, your own
Will has to answer; child, it lies

Within your power of choosing to
Conceive the Child who chooses you.

IV

SOLO AND CHORUS

Let number and weight rejoice.
In this hour of their translation
Into conscious happiness:
For the whole in every part,
The truth at the proper centre
(There's a Way. There's a Voice.)
Of language and distress
Is recognized in her heart
Singing and dancing.

Let even the great rejoice.
Though buffeted by admirers
And arrogant as noon,
The rich and the lovely have seen
For an infinitesimal moment
(There's a Way. There's a Voice.)
In another's eye till their own
Reflection came between,
Singing and dancing.

Let even the small rejoice.
Though threatened from purple rostra
And dazed by the soldier's drum
Proclaiming total defeat,
The general loquacious Public
(There's a Way. There's a Voice.)

Have been puzzled and struck dumb,
Hearing in every street
Singing and dancing.

Let even the young rejoice.
Lovers at their betrayal
Weeping alone in the night,
Have fallen asleep as they heard,
Though too far off to be certain
(There's a Way. There's a Voice.)
They had not imagined it,
Sounds that made grief absurd,
Singing and dancing.

Let even the old rejoice.
The Bleak and the Dim, abandoned
By impulse and regret,
Are startled out of their lives;
For to footsteps long expected
(There's a Way. There's a Voice.)
Their ruins echo, yet
The Demolisher arrives
Singing and dancing.

THE TEMPTATION OF ST. JOSEPH

I

JOSEPH

My shoes were shined, my pants were cleaned and pressed,
And I was hurrying to meet
    My own true Love:

But a great crowd grew and grew
Till I could not push my way through,
    Because
A star had fallen down the street;
    When they saw who I was,
The police tried to do their best.

CHORUS [*off*]

Joseph, you have heard
What Mary says occurred;
Yes, it may be so.
Is it likely? No.

JOSEPH

The bar was gay, the lighting well-designed,
And I was sitting down to wait
    My own true Love:
A voice I'd heard before, I think,
Cried: "This is on the House. I drink
    To him
Who does not know it is too late";
    When I asked for the time,
Everyone was very kind.

CHORUS [*off*]

Mary may be pure,
But, Joseph, are you sure?
How is one to tell?
Suppose, for instance ... Well ...

JOSEPH

Through cracks, up ladders, into waters deep,
I squeezed, I climbed, I swam to save
    My own true Love:

Under a dead apple tree
I saw an ass; when it saw me
    It brayed;
A hermit sat in the mouth of a cave:
    When I asked him the way,
He pretended to be asleep.

CHORUS [*off*]

Maybe, maybe not.
But, Joseph, you know what
Your world, of course, will say
About you anyway.

JOSEPH

Where are you, Father, where?
Caught in the jealous trap
Of an empty house I hear
As I sit alone in the dark
Everything, everything,
The drip of the bathroom tap,
The creak of the sofa spring,
The wind in the air-shaft, all
Making the same remark
Stupidly, stupidly,
Over and over again.
Father, what have I done?
Answer me, Father, how
Can I answer the tactless wall
Or the pompous furniture now?
Answer them ...

GABRIEL

No, you must.

JOSEPH

How then am I to know,
Father, that you are just?
Give me one reason.

GABRIEL

No.

JOSEPH

All I ask is one
Important and elegant proof
That what my Love had done
Was really at your will
And that your will is Love.

GABRIEL

No, you must believe;
Be silent, and sit still.

II

NARRATOR

For the perpetual excuse
Of Adam for his fall—"My little Eve,
God bless her, did beguile me and I ate,"
    For his insistence on a nurse,
All service, breast, and lap, for giving Fate
Feminine gender to make girls believe
That they can save him, you must now atone,
    Joseph, in silence and alone;
While she who loves you makes you shake with fright,
Your love for her must tuck you up and kiss good night.

For likening Love to war, for all
The pay-off lines of limericks in which
The weak resentful bar-fly shows his sting,
    For talking of their spiritual
Beauty to chorus-girls, for flattering
The features of old gorgons who are rich,
For the impudent grin and Irish charm
    That hides a cold will to do harm,
To-day the roles are altered; you must be
The Weaker Sex whose passion is passivity.

    For those delicious memories
Cigars and sips of brandy can restore
To old dried boys, for gallantry that scrawls
    In idolatrous detail and size
A symbol of aggression on toilet walls,
For having reasoned—"Woman is naturally pure
Since she has no moustache," for having said,
    "No woman has a business head,"
You must learn now that masculinity,
To Nature, is a non-essential luxury.

    Lest, finding it impossible
To judge its object now or throatily
Forgive it as eternal God forgives,
    Lust, tempted by this miracle
To more ingenious evil, should contrive
A heathen fetish from Virginity
To soothe the spiritual petulance
    Of worn-out rakes and maiden aunts,
Forgetting nothing and believing all,
You must behave as if this were not strange at all.

Without a change in look or word,
You both must act exactly as before;
Joseph and Mary shall be man and wife
   Just as if nothing had occurred.
There is one World of Nature and one Life;
Sin fractures the Vision, not the Fact; for
The Exceptional is always usual
   And the Usual exceptional.
To choose what is difficult all one's days
As if it were easy, that is faith. Joseph, praise.

III

SEMI-CHORUS

Joseph, Mary, pray for those
Misled by moonlight and the rose,
For all in our perplexity.
Lovers who hear a distant bell
That tolls from somewhere in their head
Across the valley of their dream—
"All those who love excessively
Foot or thigh or arm or face
Pursue a louche and fatuous fire
And stumble into Hell"—
Yet what can such foreboding seem
But intellectual talk
So long as bodies walk
An earth where Time and Space
Turn Heaven to a finite bed
And Love into desire?
Pray for us, enchanted with

The Green Bohemia of that myth
Where knowledge of the flesh can take
The guilt of being born away,
Simultaneous passions make
One eternal chastity:
Pray for us romantics, pray.

BOYS' SEMI-CHORUS

Joseph, Mary, pray for us,
Independent embryos who,
Unconscious in another, do
Evil as each creature does
In every definite decision
To improve; for even in
The germ-cell's primary division
Innocence is lost and sin,
Already given as a fact,
Once more issues as an act.

SEMI-CHORUS

Joseph, Mary, pray for all
The proper and conventional
Of whom this world approves.
Pray for those whose married loves
Acquire so readily
The indolent fidelity
Of unaired beds, for us to whom
Domestic hatred can become
A habit-forming drug, whose will
To civil anarchy
Uses disease to disobey
And makes our private bodies ill.
O pray for our salvation

Who take the prudent way,
Believing we shall be exempted
From the general condemnation
Because our self-respect is tempted
To incest not adultery:
O pray for us, the bourgeoisie.

BOYS' SEMI-CHORUS

Joseph, Mary, pray
For us children as in play
Upon the nursery floor
We gradually explore
Our members till our jealous lives
Have worked through to a clear
But trivial idea
Of that whence each derives
A vague but massive feel
Of being individual.
O pray for our redemption; for
The will that occupies
Our sensual infancy
Already is mature
And could immediately
Beget upon our flesh far more
Expressions of its disbelief
Than we shall manage to conceive
In a long life of lies.

CHORUS

Blessed Woman,
Excellent Man,
Redeem for the dull the
Average Way,

That common ungifted
Natures may
Believe that their normal
Vision can
Walk to perfection.

THE SUMMONS

I

STAR OF THE NATIVITY

I am that star most dreaded by the wise,
For they are drawn against their will to me,
Yet read in my procession through the skies
The doom of orthodox sophrosyne:
I shall discard their major preservation,
All that they know so long as no one asks;
I shall deprive them of their minor tasks
In free and legal households of sensation,
Of money, picnics, beer, and sanitation.

Beware. All those who follow me are led
Onto that Glassy Mountain where are no
Footholds for logic, to that Bridge of Dread
Where knowledge but increases vertigo:
Those who pursue me take a twisting lane
To find themselves immediately alone
With savage water or unfeeling stone,
In labyrinths where they must entertain
Confusion, cripples, tigers, thunder, pain.

THE FIRST WISE MAN

To break down Her defenses
    And profit from the vision
That plain men can predict through an
    Ascesis of their senses,
    With rack and screw I put Nature through
    A thorough inquisition:
But She was so afraid that if I were disappointed
I should hurt Her more that Her answers were disjointed—
    I did. I didn't. I will. I won't.
She is just as big a liar, in fact, as we are.
    To discover how to be truthful now
    Is the reason I follow this star.

THE SECOND WISE MAN

My faith that in Time's constant
    Flow lay real assurance
Broke down on this analysis—
    At any given instant
All solids dissolve, no wheels revolve,
    And facts have no endurance—
And who knows if it is by design or pure inadvertence
That the Present destroys its inherited self-importance?
    With envy, terror, rage, regret,
We anticipate or remember but never are.
    To discover how to be living now
    Is the reason I follow this star.

THE THIRD WISE MAN

Observing how myopic
    Is the Venus of the Soma,
The concept Ought would make, I thought,

Our passions philanthropic,
And rectify in the sensual eye
Both lens-flare and lens-coma:
But arriving at the Greatest Good by introspection
And counting the Greater Number, left no time for affection,
Laughter, kisses, squeezing, smiles:
And I learned why the learned are as despised as they are.
To discover how to be loving now
Is the reason I follow this star.

THE THREE WISE MEN

The weather has been awful,
The countryside is dreary,
Marsh, jungle, rock; and echoes mock,
Calling our hope unlawful;
But a silly song can help along
Yours ever and sincerely:
At least we know for certain that we are three old sinners,
That this journey is much too long, that we want our dinners,
And miss our wives, our books, our dogs,
But have only the vaguest idea why we are what we are.
To discover how to be human now
Is the reason we follow this star.

STAR OF THE NATIVITY

Descend into the fosse of Tribulation,
Take the cold hand of Terror for a guide;
Below you in its swirling desolation
Hear tortured Horror roaring for a bride:
O do not falter at the last request
But, as the huge deformed head rears to kill,
Answer its craving with a clear I Will;

Then wake, a child in the rose-garden, pressed
Happy and sobbing to your lover's breast.

II

NARRATOR

Now let the wife look up from her stove, the husband
Interrupt his work, the child put down its toy,
That His voice may be heard in our Just Society
    Who under the sunlight
Of His calm, possessing the good earth, do well. Pray
Silence for Caesar: stand motionless and hear
In a concourse of body and concord of soul
    His proclamation.

RECITATIVE

CITIZENS OF THE EMPIRE, GREETING. ALL MALE PERSONS
WHO SHALL HAVE ATTAINED THE AGE OF TWENTY-ONE
YEARS OR OVER MUST PROCEED IMMEDIATELY TO THE
VILLAGE, TOWNSHIP, CITY, PRECINCT OR OTHER LOCAL
ADMINISTRATIVE AREA IN WHICH THEY WERE BORN AND
THERE REGISTER THEMSELVES AND THEIR DEPENDANTS IF
ANY WITH THE POLICE. WILFUL FAILURE TO COMPLY WITH
THIS ORDER IS PUNISHABLE BY CONFISCATION OF GOODS
AND LOSS OF CIVIL RIGHTS.

NARRATOR

You have been listening to the voice of Caesar
Who overcame implacable Necessity
By His endurance and by His skill has subdued the
    Welter of Fortune.

It is meet, therefore, that, before dispersing
In pious equanimity to obey His orders,
With well-tuned instruments and grateful voices
   We should praise Caesar.

III

FUGAL-CHORUS

Great is Caesar: He has conquered Seven Kingdoms.
The First was the Kingdom of Abstract Idea:
Last night it was Tom, Dick and Harry; to-night it is S's with P's;
Instead of inflexions and accents
There are prepositions and word-order;
Instead of aboriginal objects excluding each other
There are specimens reiterating a type;
Instead of wood-nymphs and river-demons,
There is one unconditioned ground of Being.
Great is Caesar: God must be with Him.

Great is Caesar: He has conquered Seven Kingdoms.
The Second was the Kingdom of Natural Cause:
Last night it was Sixes and Sevens: to-night it is One and Two;
Instead of saying, "Strange are the whims of the Strong,"
We say, "Harsh is the Law but it is certain";
Instead of building temples, we build laboratories;
Instead of offering sacrifices, we perform experiments;
Instead of reciting prayers, we note pointer-readings;
Our lives are no longer erratic but efficient.
Great is Caesar: God must be with Him.

Great is Caesar: He has conquered Seven Kingdoms.
The Third was the Kingdom of Infinite Number:

Last night it was Rule-of-Thumb, to-night it is To-a-T;
Instead of Quite-a-lot, there is Exactly-so-many;
Instead of Only-a-few, there is Just-these;
Instead of saying, "You must wait until I have counted,"
We say, "Here you are. You will find this answer correct";
Instead of nodding acquaintance with a few integers,
The Transcendentals are our personal friends.
Great is Caesar: God must be with Him.

Great is Caesar: He has conquered Seven Kingdoms.
The Fourth was the Kingdom of Credit Exchange:
Last night it was Tit-for-Tat, to-night it is C.O.D.;
When we have a surplus, we need not meet someone with a deficit;
When we have a deficit, we need not meet someone with a surplus;
Instead of heavy treasures, there are paper symbols of value;
Instead of Pay at Once, there is Pay when you can;
Instead of My Neighbour, there is Our Customers;
Instead of Country Fair, there is World Market.
Great is Caesar: God must be with Him.

Great is Caesar: He has conquered Seven Kingdoms.
The Fifth was the Kingdom of Inorganic Giants:
Last night it was Heave-Ho, to-night it is Whee-Spree;
When we want anything, They make it;
When we dislike anything, They change it;
When we want to go anywhere, They carry us;
When the Barbarian invades us, They raise immovable shields;
When we invade the Barbarian, They brandish irresistible swords;
Fate is no longer a fiat of Matter, but a freedom of Mind.
Great is Caesar: God must be with Him.

Great is Caesar: He has conquered Seven Kingdoms.
The Sixth was the Kingdom of Organic Dwarfs:

Last night it was Ouch-Ouch, to-night it is Yum-Yum;
When diseases waylay us, They strike them dead;
When worries intrude on us, They throw them out;
When pain accosts us, They save us from embarrassment;
When we feel like sheep, They make us lions;
When we feel like geldings, They make us stallions;
Spirit is no longer under Flesh, but on top.
Great is Caesar: God must be with Him.

Great is Caesar: He has conquered Seven Kingdoms.
The Seventh was the Kingdom of Popular Soul:
Last night it was Order-Order, to-night it is Hear-Hear;
When he says, You are happy, we laugh;
When he says, You are wretched, we cry;
When he says, It is true, everyone believes it;
When he says, It is false, no one believes it;
When he says, This is good, this is loved;
When he says, That is bad, that is hated.
Great is Caesar: God must be with Him.

IV

NARRATOR

These are stirring times for the editors of newspapers:
History is in the making; Mankind is on the march.
The longest aqueduct in the world is already
Under construction; the Committees on Fen-Drainage
And Soil-Conservation will issue very shortly
Their Joint Report; even the problems of Trade Cycles
And Spiralling Prices are regarded by the experts
As practically solved; and the recent restrictions
Upon aliens and free-thinking Jews are beginning

To have a salutary effect upon public morale.
True, the Western seas are still infested with pirates,
And the rising power of the Barbarian in the North
Is giving some cause for uneasiness; but we are fully
Alive to these dangers; we are rapidly arming; and both
Will be taken care of in due course: then, united
In a sense of common advantage and common right,
Our great Empire shall be secure for a thousand years.

   If we were never alone or always too busy,
Perhaps we might even believe what we know is not true:
But no one is taken in, at least not all of the time;
In our bath, or the subway, or the middle of the night,
We know very well we are not unlucky but evil,
That the dream of a Perfect State or No State at all,
To which we fly for refuge, is a part of our punishment.
   Let us therefore be contrite but without anxiety,
For Powers and Times are not gods but mortal gifts from God;
Let us acknowledge our defeats but without despair,
For all societies and epochs are transient details,
Transmitting an everlasting opportunity
That the Kingdom of Heaven may come, not in our present
And not in our future, but in the Fullness of Time.
Let us pray.

V

CHORALE

Our Father, whose creative Will
Asked Being for us all,
Confirm it that Thy Primal Love
May weave in us the freedom of

The actually deficient on
    The justly actual.

Though written by Thy children with
    A smudged and crooked line,
Thy Word is ever legible,
Thy Meaning unequivocal,
And for Thy Goodness even sin
    Is valid as a sign.

Inflict Thy promises with each
    Occasion of distress,
That from our incoherence we
May learn to put our trust in Thee,
And brutal fact persuade us to
    Adventure, Art, and Peace.

THE VISION OF THE SHEPHERDS

I

THE FIRST SHEPHERD

The winter night requires our constant attention,
    Watching that water and good-will,
Warmth and well-being, may still be there in the morning.

THE SECOND SHEPHERD

    For behind the spontaneous joy of life
There is always a mechanism to keep going,

THE THIRD SHEPHERD

And someone like us is always there.

THE FIRST SHEPHERD

We observe that those who assure us their education
    And money would do us such harm,
How real we are just as we are, and how they envy us,
    For it is the centreless tree
And the uncivilised robin who are the truly happy,
    Have done pretty well for themselves:

THE SECOND SHEPHERD

Nor can we help noticing how those who insist that
    We ought to stand up for our rights,
And how important we are, keep insisting also
    That it doesn't matter a bit
If one of us gets arrested or injured, for
    It is only our numbers that count.

THE THIRD SHEPHERD

In a way they are right,

THE FIRST SHEPHERD

              But to behave like a cogwheel
When one knows one is no such thing,

THE SECOND SHEPHERD

Merely to add to a crowd with one's passionate body,
    Is not a virtue.

THE THIRD SHEPHERD

    What is real
About us all is that each of us is waiting.

THE FIRST SHEPHERD

    That is why we are able to bear

Ready-made clothes, second-hand art and opinions
   And being washed and ordered about;

THE SECOND SHEPHERD

That is why you should not take our conversation
   Too seriously, nor read too much
Into our songs;

THE THIRD SHEPHERD

     Their purpose is mainly to keep us
From watching the clock all the time.

THE FIRST SHEPHERD

For, though we cannot say why, we know that something
   Will happen:

THE SECOND SHEPHERD

    What we cannot say,

THE THIRD SHEPHERD

Except that it will not be a reporter's item
   Of unusual human interest;

THE FIRST SHEPHERD

That always means something unpleasant.

THE SECOND SHEPHERD

                        But one day or
The next we shall hear the Good News.

II

THE THREE SHEPHERDS

Levers nudge the aching wrist:
  "You are free
  Not to be,
  Why exist?"
Wheels a thousand times a minute
  Mutter, stutter,
"End the self you cannot mend,
Did you, friend, begin it?"
  And the streets
  Sniff at our defeats.
Then who is the Unknown
Who answers for our fear
As if it were His own,
So that we reply
Till the day we die:
"No, I don't know why,
But I'm glad I'm here"?

III

CHORUS OF ANGELS

Unto you a Child,
A Son is given.
Praising, proclaiming
The ingression of Love,
Earth's darkness invents
The blaze of Heaven,
And frigid silence

Meditates a song;
For great joy has filled
The narrow and the sad,
While the emphasis
Of the rough and big,
The abiding crag
And wandering wave,
Is on forgiveness:
Sing Glory to God
And good-will to men,
All, all, all of them.
Run to Bethlehem.

SHEPHERDS

Let us run to learn
How to love and run;
Let us run to Love.

CHORUS

Now all things living,
Domestic or wild,
With whom you must share
Light, water, and air,
And suffer and shake
In physical need,
The sullen limpet,
The exuberant weed,
The mischievous cat,
And the timid bird,
Are glad for your sake
As the new-born Word
Declares that the old
Authoritarian

Constraint is replaced
By His Covenant,
And a city based
On love and consent
Suggested to men,
All, all, all of them.
Run to Bethlehem.

SHEPHERDS

Let us run to learn
How to love and run;
Let us run to Love.

CHORUS

The primitive dead
Progress in your blood,
And generations
Of the unborn, all
Are leaping for joy
In your reins to-day
When the Many shall,
Once in your common
Certainty of this
Child's loveableness,
Resemble the One,
That after to-day
The children of men
May be certain that
The Father Abyss
Is affectionate
To all Its creatures,
All, all, all of them.
Run to Bethlehem.

AT THE MANGER

I

MARY

O shut your bright eyes that mine must endanger
With their watchfulness; protected by its shade
Escape from my care: what can you discover
From my tender look but how to be afraid?
Love can but confirm the more it would deny.
   Close your bright eye.

Sleep. What have you learned from the womb that bore you
But an anxiety your Father cannot feel?
Sleep. What will the flesh that I gave do for you,
Or my mother love, but tempt you from His will?
Why was I chosen to teach His Son to weep?
   Little One, sleep.

Dream. In human dreams earth ascends to Heaven
Where no one need pray nor ever feel alone.
In your first few hours of life here, O have you
Chosen already what death must be your own?
How soon will you start on the Sorrowful Way?
   Dream while you may.

II

FIRST WISE MAN

   Led by the light of an unusual star,
   We hunted high and low.

SECOND WISE MAN

Have travelled far,
For many days, a little group alone
With doubts, reproaches, boredom, the unknown.

THIRD WISE MAN

Through stifling gorges.

FIRST WISE MAN

Over level lakes,

SECOND WISE MAN

Tundras intense and irresponsive seas.

THIRD WISE MAN

In vacant crowds and humming silences,

FIRST WISE MAN

By ruined arches and past modern shops,

SECOND WISE MAN

Counting the miles,

THIRD WISE MAN

And the absurd mistakes.

THE THREE WISE MEN

O here and now our endless journey stops.

FIRST SHEPHERD

We never left the place where we were born,

SECOND SHEPHERD

Have lived only one day, but every day,

THIRD SHEPHERD

Have walked a thousand miles yet only worn
The grass between our work and home away.

FIRST SHEPHERD

Lonely we were though never left alone.

SECOND SHEPHERD

The solitude familiar to the poor
Is feeling that the family next door,
The way it talks, eats, dresses, loves, and hates,
Is indistinguishable from one's own.

THIRD SHEPHERD

To-night for the first time the prison gates
Have opened.

FIRST SHEPHERD

Music and sudden light

SECOND SHEPHERD

Have interrupted the routine to-night,

THIRD SHEPHERD

And swept the filth of habit from our hearts.

THE THREE SHEPHERDS

O here and now our endless journey starts.

WISE MEN

Our arrogant longing to attain the tomb,

SHEPHERDS

Our sullen wish to go back to the womb,

WISE MEN

To have no past,

SHEPHERDS

No future,

TUTTI

       Is refused.
And yet, without our knowledge, Love has used
Our weakness as a guard and guide.
                We bless

WISE MEN

Our lives' impatience,

SHEPHERDS

Our lives' laziness,

TUTTI

And bless each other's sin, exchanging here

WISE MEN

Exceptional conceit

SHEPHERDS

With average fear.

TUTTI

Released by Love from isolating wrong,
Let us for Love unite our various song,
Each with his gift according to his kind
Bringing this child his body and his mind.

III

WISE MEN

Child, at whose birth we would do obsequy
For our tall errors of imagination,
Redeem our talents with your little cry.

SHEPHERDS

Clinging like sheep to the earth for protection,
We have not ventured far in any direction:
    Wean, Child, our ageing flesh away
    From its childish way.

WISE MEN

Love is more serious than Philosophy
Who sees no humour in her observation
That Truth is knowing that we know we lie.

SHEPHERDS

When, to escape what our memories are thinking,
We go out at nights and stay up drinking,
    Stay then with our sick pride and mind
    The forgetful mind.

WISE MEN

Love does not will enraptured apathy;
Fate plays the passive role of dumb temptation
To wills where Love can doubt, affirm, deny.

SHEPHERDS

When, chafing at the rule of old offences,
We run away to the sea of the senses,
    On strange beds then O welcome home
    Our horror of home.

WISE MEN

Love knows of no somatic tyranny;
For homes are built for Love's accommodation
By bodies from the void they occupy.

SHEPHERDS

When, exhausting our wills with our evil courses,
We demand the good-will of cards and horses,
    Be then our lucky certainty
    Of uncertainty.

WISE MEN

Love does not fear substantial anarchy,
But vividly expresses obligation
With movement and in spontaneity.

SHEPHERDS

When, feeling the great boots of the rich on our faces,
We live in the hope of one day changing places,
    Be then the truth of our abuse
    That we abuse.

WISE MEN

The singular is not Love's enemy;
Love's possibilities of realisation
Require an Otherness that can say *I*.

SHEPHERDS

When in dreams the beasts and cripples of resentment
Rampage and revel to our hearts' contentment,
    Be then the poetry of hate
    That replaces hate.

WISE MEN

Not In but With our time Love's energy
Exhibits Love's immediate operation;
The choice to love is open till we die.

SHEPHERDS

O Living Love, by your birth we are able
Not only, like the ox and ass of the stable,
    To love with our live wills, but love,
    Knowing we love.

TUTTI

O Living Love replacing phantasy,
O Joy of life revealed in Love's creation;
Our mood of longing turns to indication:
Space is the Whom our loves are needed by,
Time is our choice of How to love and Why.

THE MEDITATION OF SIMEON

SIMEON

As long as the apple had not been entirely digested, as long as there remained the least understanding between Adam and the stars, rivers and horses with whom he had once known complete intimacy, as long as Eve could share in any way with the moods of the rose or the ambitions of the swallow, there was still a hope that the effects of the poison would wear off, that the exile from Paradise was only a bad dream, that the Fall had not occurred in fact.

CHORUS

When we woke, it was day; we went on weeping.

SIMEON

As long as there were any roads to amnesia and anaesthesia still to be explored, any rare wine or curiosity of cuisine as yet untested, any erotic variation as yet unimagined or unrealised, any method of torture as yet undevised, any style of conspicuous waste as yet unindulged, any eccentricity of mania or disease as yet unrepresented, there was still a hope that man had not been poisoned but transformed, that Paradise was not an eternal state from which he had been forever expelled, but a childish state which he had permanently outgrown, that the Fall had occurred by necessity.

CHORUS

We danced in the dark, but were not deceived.

SIMEON

As long as there were any experiments still to be undertaken in restoring that order in which desire had once rejoiced to be reflected, any code of equity and obligation upon which some society had not yet been founded, any species of property of which the value had not yet been appreciated, any talent that had not yet won private devotion and public honour, any rational concept of the Good or intuitive feeling for the Holy that had not yet found its precise and beautiful expression, any technique of contemplation or ritual of sacrifice and praise that had not yet been properly conducted, any faculty of mind or body that had not yet been thoroughly disciplined, there was still a hope that some antidote might be found, that the gates of Paradise had indeed slammed to, but with the exercise of a little patience and ingenuity could be unlocked, that the Fall had occurred by accident.

CHORUS

Lions came loping into the lighted city.

SIMEON

Before the Positive could manifest Itself specifically, it was necessary that nothing should be left that negation could remove; the emancipation of Time from Space had first to be complete, the Revolution of the Images, in which the memories rose up and cast into subjection the senses by Whom hitherto they had been enslaved, successful beyond their wildest dreams, the mirror in which the Soul expected to admire herself so perfectly polished that her natural consolation of vagueness should be utterly withdrawn.

CHORUS

We looked at our Shadow, and, Lo, it was lame.

SIMEON

Before the Infinite could manifest Itself in the finite, it was necessary that man should first have reached that point along his road to Knowledge where, just as it rises from the swamps of Confusion onto the sunny slopes of Objectivity, it forks in opposite directions towards the One and the Many; where, therefore, in order to proceed at all, he must decide which is Real and which only Appearance, yet at the same time cannot escape the knowledge that his choice is arbitrary and subjective.

CHORUS

Promising to meet, we parted forever.

SIMEON

Before the Unconditional could manifest Itself under the conditions of existence, it was necessary that man should first have reached the ultimate frontier of consciousness, the secular limit of memory beyond which there remained but one thing for him to know, his Original Sin, but of this it is impossible for him to become conscious because it is itself what conditions his will to knowledge. For as long as he was in Paradise he could not sin by any conscious intention or act: his as yet unfallen will could only rebel against the truth by taking flight into an unconscious lie; he could only eat of the Tree of Knowledge of Good and Evil by forgetting that its existence was a fiction of the Evil One, that there is only the Tree of Life.

CHORUS

The bravest drew back on the brink of the Abyss.

SIMEON

From the beginning until now God spoke through his prophets. The Word aroused the uncomprehending depths of their flesh to a witnessing fury, and their witness was this: that the Word should be made Flesh. Yet their witness could only be received as long as it was vaguely misunderstood, as long as it seemed either to be neither impossible nor necessary, or necessary but not impossible, or impossible but not necessary; and the prophecy could not therefore be fulfilled. For it could only be fulfilled when it was no longer possible to receive, because it was clearly understood as absurd. The Word could not be made Flesh until men had reached a state of absolute contradiction between clarity and despair in which they would have no choice but either to accept absolutely or to reject absolutely, yet in their choice there should be no element of luck, for they would be fully conscious of what they were accepting or rejecting.

CHORUS

The eternal spaces were congested and depraved.

SIMEON

But here and now the Word which is implicit in the Beginning and in the End is become immediately explicit, and that which hitherto we could only passively fear as the incomprehensible I AM, henceforth we may actively love with comprehension that THOU ART. Wherefore, having seen Him, not in some prophetic vision of what might be, but with the eyes of our own weakness as to what actually is, we are bold to say that we have seen our salvation.

CHORUS

Now and forever, we are not alone.

SIMEON

By the event of this birth the true significance of all other events is defined, for of every other occasion it can be said that it could have been different, but of this birth it is the case that it could in no way be other than it is. And by the existence of this Child, the proper value of all other existences is given, for of every other creature it can be said that it has extrinsic importance but of this Child it is the case that He is in no sense a symbol.

CHORUS

We have right to believe that we really exist.

By Him is dispelled the darkness wherein the fallen will cannot distinguish between temptation and sin, for in Him we become fully conscious of Necessity as our freedom to be tempted, and of Freedom as our necessity to have faith. And by Him is illuminated the time in which we execute those choices through which our freedom is realized or prevented, for the course of History is predictable in the degree to which all men love themselves, and spontaneous in the degree to which each man loves God and through Him his neighbour.

CHORUS

The distresses of choice are our chance to be blessed.

SIMEON

Because in Him the Flesh is united to the Word without magical transformation, Imagination is redeemed from promiscuous fornication with her own images. The tragic conflict of Virtue with Necessity is no longer confined to the Exceptional Hero; for disaster is not the impact of a curse upon a few great families, but issues continually from the hubris of every tainted will. Every invalid is Roland defending the narrow pass against hopeless odds, every stenographer Brünnhilde refusing to renounce her lover's ring which came into existence through the renunciation of love.

Nor is the Ridiculous a species any longer of the Ugly; for since of themselves all men are without merit, all are ironically assisted to their comic bewilderment by the Grace of God. Every Cabinet Minister is the woodcutter's simple-minded son to whom the fishes and the crows are always whispering the whereabouts of the Dancing Water or the Singing Branch, every heiress the washerwoman's butter-fingered daughter on whose pillow the fairy keeps laying the herb that could cure the Prince's mysterious illness.

Nor is there any situation which is essentially more or less interesting than another. Every tea-table is a battlefield littered with old catastrophes and haunted by the vague ghosts of vast issues, every martyrdom an occasion for flip cracks and sententious oratory.

Because in Him all passions find a logical In-Order-That, by Him is the perpetual recurrence of Art assured.

CHORUS

Safe in His silence, our songs are at play.

SIMEON

Because in Him the Word is united to the Flesh without loss of perfection, Reason is redeemed from incestuous fixation on her own Logic, for the One and the Many are simultaneously revealed as real. So that we may no longer, with the Barbarians, deny the Unity, asserting that there are as many gods as there are creatures, nor, with the philosophers, deny the Multiplicity, asserting that God is One who has no need of friends and is indifferent to a World of Time and Quantity and Horror which He did not create, nor, with Israel, may we limit the co-inherence of the One and the Many to a special case, asserting that God is only concerned with and of concern to that People whom out of all that He created He has chosen for His own.

For the Truth is indeed One, without which is no salvation, but the possibilities of real knowledge are as many as are the creatures in the very real and most exciting universe that God creates with and for His love, and it is not Nature which is one public illusion, but we who have each our many private illusions about Nature.

Because in Him abstraction finds a passionate For-The-Sake-Of, by Him is the continuous development of Science assured.

CHORUS

Our lost Appearances are saved by His love.

SIMEON

And because of His visitation, we may no longer desire God as if He were lacking: our redemption is no longer a question of pursuit but of surrender to Him who is always and everywhere present. Therefore at every moment we pray that, following Him, we may depart from our anxiety into His peace.

CHORUS

Its errors forgiven, may our Vision come home.

THE MASSACRE OF THE INNOCENTS

I

HEROD

Because I am bewildered, because I must decide, because my decision must be in conformity with Nature and Necessity, let me honour those through whom my nature is by necessity what it is.

To Fortune—that I have become Tetrarch, that I have escaped assassination, that at sixty my head is clear and my digestion sound.

To my Father—for the means to gratify my love of travel and study.

To my Mother—for a straight nose.

To Eva, my coloured nurse—for regular habits.

To my brother, Sandy, who married a trapeze artist and died of drink—for so refuting the position of the Hedonists.

To Mr. Stewart, nicknamed The Carp, who instructed me in the elements of geometry through which I came to perceive the errors of the tragic poets.

To Professor Lighthouse—for his lectures on The Peloponnesian War.

To the stranger on the boat to Sicily—for recommending to me Brown on Resolution.

To my secretary, Miss Button—for admitting that my speeches were inaudible.

There is no visible disorder. No crime—what could be more innocent than the birth of an artisan's child? To-day has been one of those perfect winter days, cold, brilliant, and utterly still, when the bark of the shepherd's dog carries for miles, and the great wild mountains come up quite close to the city walls, and the mind feels intensely awake, and this evening as I stand at this window high up in the citadel there is nothing in the whole magnificent panorama of plain and mountains to indicate that the Empire is threatened by a danger more dreadful than any invasion of Tartars on racing camels or conspiracy of the Praetorian Guard.

Barges are unloading soil fertiliser at the river wharves. Soft drinks and sandwiches may be had in the inns at reasonable prices. Allotment gardening has become popular. The highway to the coast goes straight up over the mountains and the truck-drivers no longer carry guns. Things are beginning to take shape. It is a long time since anyone stole the park benches or murdered the swans. There are children in this province who have never seen a louse, shopkeepers who have never handled a counterfeit coin, women of forty who have never hidden in a ditch except for fun. Yes, in twenty years I have managed to do a little. Not enough, of course. There are villages only a few miles from here where they still believe in witches. There isn't a single town where a good bookshop would pay. One could count on the fingers of one hand the people capable of solving the problem of Achilles and the Tortoise. Still it is a beginning. In twenty years the darkness has been pushed back a few inches. And what, after all, is the whole Empire, with its few thousand square miles on which it is possible to lead the Rational Life, but a tiny patch of light compared with those immense areas of barbaric night that surround it on all sides, that incoherent wilderness of rage and terror, where Mongolian idiots are regarded as sacred and mothers who give birth to twins are instantly put to death, where malaria is treated by yelling, where warriors of superb courage obey the commands of hysterical female impersonators, where the best cuts of meat are reserved for the dead, where, if a white blackbird has been seen, no more work may be done that day, where it is firmly believed that the world was created by a giant with three heads or that the motions of the stars are controlled from the liver of a rogue elephant?

Yet even inside this little civilized patch itself, where, at the cost of heaven knows how much grief and bloodshed, it has been made unnecessary for anyone over the age of twelve to believe in fairies or that First Causes reside in mortal and finite objects, so many are still homesick for that disorder wherein every passion formerly enjoyed a frantic license. Caesar flies to his hunting lodge pursued by ennui; in the faubourgs of the Capital, Society grows savage, corrupted by silks and scents, softened by sugar and hot water, made insolent by theatres and attractive slaves; and everywhere, including this province, new prophets spring up every day to sound the old barbaric note.

I have tried everything. I have prohibited the sale of crystals and ouija-boards; I have slapped a heavy tax on playing cards; the courts are empowered to sentence alchemists to hard labour in the mines; it is a statutory offense to turn tables or feel bumps. But nothing is really effective. How can I expect the masses to be sensible when, for instance, to my certain knowledge, the captain of my own guard wears an amulet against the Evil Eye, and the richest merchant in the city consults a medium over every important transaction?

Legislation is helpless against the wild prayer of longing that rises, day in, day out, from all these households under my protection: "O God, put away justice and truth for we cannot understand them and do not want them. Eternity would bore us dreadfully. Leave Thy heav-

ens and come down to our earth of waterclocks and hedges. Become
our uncle. Look after Baby, amuse Grandfather, escort Madam to the
Opera, help Willy with his home-work, introduce Muriel to a hand-
some naval officer. Be interesting and weak like us, and we will love
you as we love ourselves."

Reason is helpless, and now even the Poetic Compromise no longer
works, all those lovely fairy tales in which Zeus, disguising himself as a
swan or a bull or a shower of rain or what-have-you, lay with some
beautiful woman and begot a hero. For the Public has grown too so-
phisticated. Under all the charming metaphors and symbols, it de-
tects the stern command, "Be and act heroically"; behind the myth of
divine origin, it senses the real human excellence that is a reproach to
its own baseness. So, with a bellow of rage, it kicks Poetry downstairs
and sends for Prophecy. "Your sister has just insulted me. I asked for a
God who should be as like me as possible. What use to me is a God
whose divinity consists in doing difficult things that I cannot do or
saying clever things that I cannot understand? The God I want and
intend to get must be someone I can recognise immediately without
having to wait and see what he says or does. There must be nothing in
the least extraordinary about him. Produce him at once, please. I'm
sick of waiting."

To-day, apparently, judging by the trio who came to see me this
morning with an ecstatic grin on their scholarly faces, the job has
been done. "God has been born," they cried, "we have seen him our-
selves. The World is saved. Nothing else matters."

One needn't be much of a psychologist to realise that if this rumour
is not stamped out now, in a few years it is capable of diseasing the
whole Empire, and one doesn't have to be a prophet to predict the
consequences if it should.

Reason will be replaced by Revelation. Instead of Rational Law, ob-
jective truths perceptible to any who will undergo the necessary intel-
lectual discipline, and the same for all, Knowledge will degenerate

into a riot of subjective visions—feelings in the solar plexus induced by undernourishment, angelic images generated by fevers or drugs, dream warnings inspired by the sound of falling water. Whole cosmogonies will be created out of some forgotten personal resentment, complete epics written in private languages, the daubs of school children ranked above the greatest masterpieces.

Idealism will be replaced by Materialism. Priapus will only have to move to a good address and call himself Eros to become the darling of middle-aged women. Life after death will be an eternal dinner party where all the guests are twenty years old. Diverted from its normal and wholesome outlet in patriotism and civic or family pride, the need of the materialistic Masses for some visible Idol to worship will be driven into totally unsocial channels where no education can reach it. Divine honours will be paid to silver tea-pots, shallow depressions in the earth, names on maps, domestic pets, ruined windmills, even in extreme cases, which will become increasingly common, to headaches, or malignant tumors, or four o'clock in the afternoon.

Justice will be replaced by Pity as the cardinal human virtue, and all fear of retribution will vanish. Every corner-boy will congratulate himself: "I'm such a sinner that God had to come down in person to save me. I must be a devil of a fellow." Every crook will argue: "I like committing crimes. God likes forgiving them. Really the world is admirably arranged." And the ambition of every young cop will be to secure a death-bed repentance. The New Aristocracy will consist exclusively of hermits, bums, and permanent invalids. The Rough Diamond, the Consumptive Whore, the bandit who is good to his mother, the epileptic girl who has a way with animals will be the heroes and heroines of the New Tragedy when the general, the statesman, and the philosopher have become the butt of every farce and satire.

Naturally this cannot be allowed to happen. Civilisation must be saved even if this means sending for the military, as I suppose it does. How dreary. Why is it that in the end civilisation always has to call in

these professional tidiers to whom it is all one whether it be Pythago-
ras or a homicidal lunatic that they are instructed to exterminate. O
dear, Why couldn't this wretched infant be born somewhere else? Why
can't people be sensible? I don't want to be horrid. Why can't they see
that the notion of a finite God is absurd? Because it is. And suppose,
just for the sake of argument, that it isn't, that this story is true, that
this child is in some inexplicable manner both God and Man, that he
grows up, lives, and dies, without committing a single sin? Would that
make life any better? On the contrary it would make it far, far worse.
For it can only mean this: that once having shown them how, God
would expect every man, whatever his fortune, to lead a sinless life in
the flesh and on earth. Then indeed would the human race be
plunged into madness and despair. And for me personally at this mo-
ment it would mean that God had given me the power to destroy
Himself. I refuse to be taken in. He could not play such a horrible
practical joke. Why should He dislike me so? I've worked like a slave.
Ask anyone you like. I read all official dispatches without skipping.
I've taken elocution lessons. I've hardly ever taken bribes. How dare
He allow me to decide? I've tried to be good. I brush my teeth every
night. I haven't had sex for a month. I object. I'm a liberal. I want ev-
eryone to be happy. I wish I had never been born.

II

SOLDIERS

When the Sex War ended with the slaughter of the Grandmothers,
They found a bachelor's baby suffocating under them;
Somebody called him George and that was the end of it:
    They hitched him up to the Army.
    George, you old debutante,
    How did you get in the Army?

In the Retreat from Reason he deserted on his rocking-horse
And lived on a fairy's kindness till he tired of kicking her;
He smashed her spectacles and stole her

                                  cheque-book and mackintosh

     Then cruised his way back to the Army.
     George, you old numero,
     How did you get in the Army?

Before the Diet of Sugar he was using razor-blades
And exited soon after with an allergy to maidenheads;
He discovered a cure of his own, but no one would patent it,

     So he showed up again in the Army.
     George, you old flybynight,
     How did you get in the Army?

When the Vice Crusades were over he was hired by some Muscovites
Prospecting for deodorants among the Eskimos;
He was caught by a common cold and

                                    condemned to the whiskey mines,

     But schemozzled back to the Army.
     George, you old Emperor,
     How did you get in the Army?

Since Peace was signed with Honour he's been minding his business;
But, whoops, here comes His Idleness, buttoning his uniform;
Just in tidy time to massacre the Innocents;

     He's come home to roost in the Army.
     George, you old matador,
     Welcome back to the Army.

III

RACHEL

On the Left are grinning dogs, peering down into a solitude
         too deep to fill with roses.
On the Right are sensible sheep, gazing up at a pride where
         no dream can grow.
Somewhere in these unending wastes of delirium is a lost child,
       speaking of Long Ago in the language of wounds.
To-morrow, perhaps, he will come to himself in Heaven.
But here Grief turns her silence, neither in this direction, nor
         in that, nor for any reason.
And her coldness now is on the earth forever.

THE FLIGHT INTO EGYPT

I

JOSEPH

Mirror, let us through the glass
No authority can pass.

MARY

Echo, if the strong should come,
Tell a white lie or be dumb.

VOICES OF THE DESERT

It was visitors' day at the vinegar works
In Tenderloin Town when I tore my time;
A sorrowful snapshot was my sinful wage:
Was that why you left me, elusive bones?

Come to our bracing desert
Where eternity is eventful,
  For the weather-glass
  Is set at Alas,
The thermometer at Resentful.

MARY

The Kingdom of the Robbers lies
Between Time and our memories;

JOSEPH

Fugitives from Space must cross
The waste of the Anonymous.

VOICES OF THE DESERT

How should he figure my fear of the dark?
The moment he can he'll remember me,
The silly he locked in the cellar for fun,
And his dear little doggie shall die in his arms.
  Come to our old-world desert
  Where everyone goes to pieces;
    You can pick up tears
    For souvenirs
  Or genuine diseases.

JOSEPH

Geysers and volcanoes give
Sudden comical relief;

MARY

And the vulture is a boon
On a dull hot afternoon.

VOICES OF THE DESERT

All Father's nightingales knew their place,
The gardens were loyal: look at them now.
The roads are so careless, the rivers so rude,
My studs have been stolen; I must speak to the sea.

    Come to our well-run desert
    Where anguish arrives by cable,
      And the deadly sins
      May be bought by tins
    With instructions on the label.

MARY

Skulls recurring every mile
Direct the thirsty to the Nile;

JOSEPH

And the jackal's eye at night
Forces Error to keep right.

VOICES OF THE DESERT

In the land of lilies I lost my wits,
Nude as a number all night I ran
With a ghost for a guest along green canals;
By the waters of waking I wept for the weeds.

    Come to our jolly desert
    Where even the dolls go whoring;
      Where cigarette-ends
      Become intimate friends,
    And it's always three in the morning.

JOSEPH AND MARY

Safe in Egypt we shall sigh
For lost insecurity;

Only when her terrors come
Does our flesh feel quite at home.

II

RECITATIVE

Fly, Holy Family, from our immediate rage,
That our future may be freed from our past; retrace
    The footsteps of law-giving
  Moses, back through the sterile waste,

Down to the rotten kingdom of Egypt, the damp
Tired delta where in her season of glory our
    Forefathers sighed in bondage;
  Abscond with the Child to the place

That their children dare not revisit, to the time
They do not care to remember; hide from our pride
    In our humiliation;
  Fly from our death with our new life.

III

NARRATOR

Well, so that is that. Now we must dismantle the tree,
Putting the decorations back into their cardboard boxes—
Some have got broken—and carrying them up to the attic.
The holly and the mistletoe must be taken down and burnt,
And the children got ready for school. There are enough
Left-overs to do, warmed-up, for the rest of the week—
Not that we have much appetite, having drunk such a lot,

Stayed up so late, attempted—quite unsuccessfully—
To love all of our relatives, and in general
Grossly overestimated our powers. Once again
As in previous years we have seen the actual Vision and failed
To do more than entertain it as an agreeable
Possibility, once again we have sent Him away,
Begging though to remain His disobedient servant,
The promising child who cannot keep His word for long.
The Christmas Feast is already a fading memory,
And already the mind begins to be vaguely aware
Of an unpleasant whiff of apprehension at the thought
Of Lent and Good Friday which cannot, after all, now
Be very far off. But, for the time being, here we all are,
Back in the moderate Aristotelian city
Of darning and the Eight-Fifteen, where Euclid's geometry
And Newton's mechanics would account for our experience,
And the kitchen table exists because I scrub it.
It seems to have shrunk during the holidays. The streets
Are much narrower than we remembered; we had forgotten
The office was as depressing as this. To those who have seen
The Child, however dimly, however incredulously,
The Time Being is, in a sense, the most trying time of all.
For the innocent children who whispered so excitedly
Outside the locked door where they knew the presents to be
Grew up when it opened. Now, recollecting that moment
We can repress the joy, but the guilt remains conscious;
Remembering the stable where for once in our lives
Everything became a You and nothing was an It.
And craving the sensation but ignoring the cause,
We look round for something, no matter what, to inhibit
Our self-reflection, and the obvious thing for that purpose
Would be some great suffering. So, once we have met the Son,
We are tempted ever after to pray to the Father:

"Lead us into temptation and evil for our sake."
They will come, all right, don't worry; probably in a form
That we do not expect, and certainly with a force
More dreadful than we can imagine. In the meantime
There are bills to be paid, machines to keep in repair,
Irregular verbs to learn, the Time Being to redeem
From insignificance. The happy morning is over,
The night of agony still to come; the time is noon:
When the Spirit must practise his scales of rejoicing
Without even a hostile audience, and the Soul endure
A silence that is neither for nor against her faith
That God's Will be done, that, in spite of her prayers,
God will cheat no one, not even the world of its triumph.

IV

CHORUS

He is the Way.
Follow Him through the land of Unlikeness;
You will see rare beasts, and have unique adventures.

He is the Truth.
Seek Him in the Kingdom of Anxiety;
You will come to a great city that has expected your return for years.

He is the Life.
Love Him in the World of the Flesh;
And at your marriage all its occasions shall dance for joy.

TEXTUAL NOTES

ABBREVIATIONS

Berg   The Henry W. and Albert A. Berg Collection of English and American Literature at the New York Public Library.

CP   Auden, *Collected Poems*, ed. Edward Mendelson (New York: Modern Library, 2007).

HUA   Harvard University Archives

JF   John Fuller, *W. H. Auden: A Commentary* (Princeton: Princeton University Press, 1998).

LA   Edward Mendelson, *Later Auden* (New York: Farrar, Straus and Giroux, 1999).

P2   *The Complete Works of W. H. Auden: Prose: Volume II: 1939–1948*, ed. Edward Mendelson (Princeton: Princeton University Press, 2002).

P3   *The Complete Works of W. H. Auden: Prose: Volume III: 1949–1955*, ed. Edward Mendelson (Princeton: Princeton University Press, 2008).

P4   *The Complete Works of W. H. Auden: Prose: Volume IV: 1956–1962*, ed. Edward Mendelson (Princeton: Princeton University Press, 2010).

SP   Auden, *Selected Poems*, expanded edition, ed. Edward Mendelson (New York: Vintage, 2007).

T1   The first complete typescript of the poem, cited from a photocopy of the lost original once in the possession of James Stern.

T2   The second complete typescript of the poem, in the collection of the Britten-Pears Library, Aldeburgh, Suffolk, England.

In the notes that follow, the Bible is cited from the Authorized (King James) Version, since that is the one that Auden knew and used. Definitions of unusual words are adapted from the first edition of the *Oxford English Dictionary*. When I have been able to cite a published source for quotations from letters and other personal documents, I have done so. I have cited Auden's poems from the most recent edition of the *Collected Poems* when possible, though, because Auden edited some of his earlier poems rather heavily, I have sometimes had recourse to the *Selected Poems* when the original versions are preserved there.

Information about the textual history of this poem and the parts thereof—as given in these notes and in the portion of the Introduction devoted to the text of this edition—is taken from *W. H. Auden: A Bibliography, 1924–1969*, 2nd ed., by B. C. Bloomfield and Edward Mendelson (Charlottesville: University Press of Virginia, 1972).

PREFACE

Page

vii "When mother dies": Letter to Alan Ansen, October 1947 (Berg).

vii "I never really loved": Letter to James Stern of 25 April 1942, in *"In Solitude, for Company": W. H. Auden after 1940*, ed. Katherine Bucknell and Nicholas Jenkins, Auden Studies 3 (Oxford: Clarendon Press, 1995), 73–74.

viii "this round O": "In Sickness and in Health," *CP* 318.

viii "the author and giver": "At the Grave of Henry James," *SP* 132.

viii "Because it is through you": This verse letter is printed in full in *LA* 182–83.

INTRODUCTION

Page

xii "a long poem in several": *JF* 345.

xiii "I have never written": *LA* 71.

xiii "what Martin Luther called": Luther published his *De Servo Arbitrio*, or *The Bondage of the Will*, in 1525 as a refutation of Erasmus.

xiii "The Edifying in the Thought": *Either/Or: A Fragment of Life*, 2 vols., trans. David Ferdinand Swenson, Lillian Marvin Swenson, and Walter Lowrie (Princeton: Princeton University Press, 1944), 2:289.

xiii "All will be judged": *SP* 132.

xiii "Beloved, we are always": *CP* 317.

xiv "I have been reading": *P4* 30.

xiv "For the first time": *P3* 578.

xiv "dying each other's life": "Bors to Elayne: on the King's Coins," in *The Arthurian Poems of Charles Williams: Taliessen through Logres and the Region of the Summer Stars* (Cambridge: D. S. Brewer, 1938), 45. Auden quotes this passage at length at the conclusion of his essay "Brothers and Others" (*P4* 618).

xv "The conversion of time": Charles Williams, *The Descent of the Dove: A Short History of the Holy Spirit in the Church* (London: Longmans, Green and Co., 1939), 15.

xv "the method of the imposition": Williams, *The Descent of the Dove*, 117.

xvi "He begins the review": "Augustus to Augustine," *P2* 226–32.

xvii "that it was possible": Charles Norris Cochrane, *Christianity and Classical Culture: A Study of Thought and Action from Augustus to Augustine* (New York: Oxford University Press, 1940), vi.

xvii "the fall of Rome": Cochrane, *Christianity and Classical Culture*, 355.

xvii "the discovery of personality": Cochrane, *Christianity and Classical Culture*, 399.

xix "not as 'mere duration'": Tillich, *The Interpretation of History* (New York: Charles Scribner's Sons, 1936), 129. Probably in early 1941 Auden wrote a long, complex, and abstract poem, "Kairos and Logos," based on his reading of Tillich (*CP* 303).

xx "The Incarnation, the coming": *P4* 776.

xx "the clock on the mantelpiece": See page 3 below.

xxi "The violent howling": See page 7 below.

xxi "Sorry you are puzzled": Letter to George Augustus Auden, 13 October 1942 (Berg).

xxii "This is the Abomination": See page 7 below.

xxii "Where is that Law": See page 7 below.

xxii "our dreadful wood: See page 7 below.

xxii "the garden is the only": See page 8 below.

xxiii "Carry me back, Master": *CP* 436.

xxiii "Therefore, see without looking": See page 9 below.

xxiii "the greatest poet now": *P2* 182.

xxiv "Bosh, straight from Jung": See *LA* 247. The copy of Auden's 1945 *Collected Poetry* belonged to a Yale student named Robert Franklin. He was part of a group at Berkeley College who, on 16 December 1963, read an abridged version of "For the Time Being" at the apartment of Professor Frederick Watkins. (Franklin was the Narrator.) Though Auden was not present at the reading, at some time beforehand he met with Franklin and, in addition to making verbal comments about the poem, wrote instructions in Franklin's book. These involved making cuts, reassigning speeches to accommodate a reduced number of Shepherds and Wise Men, and offering suggestions about how to enunciate some of the speeches. In 1979 Franklin sent a transcript of his notes to Edward Mendelson.

Jung develops his picture of the Faculties in his *Psychologische Typen* of 1921; Auden would have read an early English edition, *Psychological Types: or, The Psychology of Individuation*, trans. H. G. Baynes, rev. R.F.C. Hull (London: Routledge and Kegan Paul, 1924).

xxiv "We who are four": See page 10 below.

xxv "What Eliot claimed": In his essay "The Metaphysical Poets," in *Selected Essays* (New York: Harcourt, Brace & World, 1950), 241–50.

xxv "Byzantium during the reign": Yeats, *A Vision* (London: Macmillan, 1937), 279–80.

xxvi "Joseph is me": Alan Ansen, *The Table Talk of W. H. Auden*, ed. Nicholas Jenkins (London: Faber & Faber, 1990), 13.

xxvi "Disjointed items stopped": See note below, page 77.

xxvi "And then, providentially": From Auden's contribution to an anthology called *Modern Canterbury Pilgrims*, reprinted in *P3* 579.

xxvii "All I ask is one": See page 21 below.

xxvii "I love him to distraction": Bucknell and Jenkins, *"In Solitude, for Company"*, 67.

xxvii "Because, although our love": *LA* 183.

xxviii "you must now atone": See page 21 below.

xxviii "common, ungifted / Natures": See page 26 below.

xxix "I am that star": See page 26 below.

xxix "In this 'fugal-chorus'": See page 30 below.

xxix "signing up for the Merchant Marine": See his letter of 13 November 1942 to James Stern, in Bucknell and Jenkins, *"In Solitude, for Company"*, 86.

xxx "It is unlikely that": Auden reviewed this collection in the *New York Times Book Review*, see *P2* 239–42.

xxx "In the year 1944": Jarrell, "Freud to Paul: The Stages of Auden's Ideology," first published in *Partisan Review* 12 (Fall 1945), reprinted in *The Third Book of Criticism* (New York: Farrar, Straus and Giroux, 1969), 153–90.

xxx "the danger is that": *P2* 153.

xxx "practically solved": See page 32 below.

xxxi "to behave like a cogwheel": See page 35 below.

xxxi "At the Manger": See page 40 below.

xxxi "never left the place": See page 41 below.

xxxii "Levers nudge the aching wrist": See page 37 below.

xxxiii "Having seen him": See page 50 below.

xxxiii "The chief reason": Letter to Spencer of 29 April 1943 (HUA). Auden continued, "Am afraid if I give the chorus more, the whole section will become disproportionately long. But I must think about this."

xxxiii "the alternative routes": From the "Caliban to the Audience" section of "The Sea and the Mirror," *CP* 440.

xxxiii "The Word could not": See page 49 below.

xxxiv "but of this Child": See page 50 below.

xxxiv "Why can't people be": See page 58 below.

xxxv "who married a trapeze artist": See page 53 below.

xxxv "I've hardly ever taken": See page 58 below.

xxxv "the moderate Aristotelian": See page 64 below.

xxxvi "It's the only direct": Ansen, *The Table Talk of W. H. Auden*, 3.

xxxvi "I have stretched out": Postcard from Ann Arbor, postmarked 11 November 1941 (Berg).

xxxvii "Ben had expected a text": Humphrey Carpenter, *W. H. Auden: A Biography* (Boston: Houghton Mifflin, 1981), 323.

FOR THE TIME BEING

Page

1 "What shall we say then?": A famous passage from Paul's letter to the Romans (6:1–2), repudiating antinomianism. The verse is echoed in John Bunyan's spiritual autobiography *Grace Abounding to the Chief of Sinners* (1666).

3 "Portly Caesar yawns": The first indication that Auden intends, throughout this poem, to use the Roman Empire as an image of all political authority.

3 "Can great Hercules": Hercules serves here as an embodiment of the Hero, a human figure in whom any given society might place its hopes for rescue from its various miseries. Auden's fullest exploration of this theme appears in *The Age of Anxiety*, in the great "Dirge" that mourns the death, or the failure ever to appear, of "some semi-divine stranger with superhuman powers, some Gilgamesh or Napoleon, some Solon or Sherlock Holmes."

4 "famishing Arachne": In Ovid's *Metamorphoses* (bk. 6) Arachne is a girl transformed by Athena into a spider, but Auden seems to be using the name—which simply means "spider" in Greek—to indicate a monstrous threat to Hercules. He sometimes wrote of his own fear of spiders, as in his poem "Plains": "spotted by spiders from afar, / I have tried to run, knowing there was no hiding and no help" (*CP* 565).

4 "tourbillions": A tourbillion is a vortex, as in a whirlpool or whirlwind.

4 "And delete the cedar grove": The typescripts (T1 and T2) read "delate" instead of "delete." According to the *OED* this verb can mean "to carry away," but also "to accuse, bring a charge against, impeach." It seems likely

that Auden intended the rarer word and either did not notice or accepted the substitution of the more common one.

5 "on account of the political situation": In his memoir *Kathleen and Frank* (New York: Simon and Schuster, 1971), Christopher Isherwood notes that at the outset of World War II, when the British government asked citizens to be "tight-lipped for security reasons," his mother, in her letters to him, eschewed the word "war" altogether. In one letter she wrote of attending a wedding where "owing to the political situation there was a large hole in the roof" (pp. 46–47).

5 "our familiar tribulations": Auden wrote to Theodore Spencer, who apparently objected to this line and some others on the same grounds, "'These after all are our familiar tribulations' and 'the exceptional conceit' are as you say too reminiscent of the Aged Eagle. Will alter them, if I can think of anything else, though I doubt if I can." The "Aged Eagle" is Eliot: "Why should the agèd eagle stretch its wings?" is a line from his 1930 poem "Ash-Wednesday."

6 "From sword to ploughshare": "And he shall judge among the nations, and shall rebuke many people: and they shall beat their swords into plowshares, and their spears into pruninghooks: nation shall not lift up sword against nation, neither shall they learn war any more" (Isaiah 2:4). The phrase is used here ironically, since in this vision of cyclical history any swords beaten into plowshares will eventually be reforged into swords.

6 "the room behind the mirror": For an explanation of Auden's thinking about mirrors, see the Introduction, p. xxv. Mirrors are an image of self-regard but also of reversal: especially in his long poem "The Sea and the Mirror" Auden uses the mirror as his key metaphor of what art does, drawing on Hamlet's claim that "the purpose of playing ... both at the first and now, was and is, to hold, as 'twere, the mirror up to nature" (3.2). The artistic mirror reverses because it is not direct representation but, when done rightly, a Kierkegaardian "indirect communication."

7 "the Abomination": "Abomination" is a word used on a number of occasions in the Bible, but the use that Auden has in mind here is probably the apocalyptic vision in Daniel 12 wherein the prophet sees "the abomination that maketh desolate." About this image Jesus would later say (Matthew 24:15–21),

> When ye therefore shall see the abomination of desolation, spoken of by Daniel the prophet, standing where it ought not, (whoso readeth, let him understand,) then let them which be in Judaea flee to the

mountains: And let him which is on the housetop not come down to take any thing out of his house: Neither let him which is in the field return back to take up his clothes. And woe to them that are with child, and to them that give suck in those days! But pray that your flight be not in the winter, neither on the sabbath day. For then shall be great tribulation, such as was not since the beginning of the world to this time, no, nor ever shall be.

That Auden has this passage about the end of things in mind is reinforced by the correspondence between Jesus's admonition "pray that your flight be not in the winter" and the refrain of the earlier chorus, "Winter completes an age."

"The wrath of God" likewise refers to a biblical apocalypse, in this case the book of Revelation (6:17): "For the great day of his wrath is come; and who shall be able to stand?"

7 "about a dreadful wood": Cf. these lines from Auden's poem "September 1, 1939" (*SP* 95):

> The lights must never go out,
> The music must always play,
> All the conventions conspire
> To make this fort assume
> The furniture of home;
> Lest we should see where we are,
> Lost in a haunted wood,
> Children afraid of the night
> Who have never been happy or good.

7 "Where is that Law": In poems of this period Auden often reflects on the paradoxical nature of the moral law, which both accuses (since we often break it) and consoles (since it indicates some unwavering principle of cosmic order). See especially the poems "Law Like Love" (*CP* 260, written in September 1939) and "The Hidden Law" (*CP* 262, written a year later).

8 "The Pilgrim Way": Especially in medieval spirituality, the life of the Christian is referred to as a pilgrimage: the Christian in this world experiences the *status viatoris*, the condition of being a wayfarer or pilgrim. (There is a "Pilgrims' Way" in England, a path leading from Winchester to Canterbury, once followed by pilgrims to the shrine of St. Thomas Becket, but so specific a reference is unlikely here.)

8 "the Abyss": Auden may have been thinking specifically of one of Nietzsche's most famous aphorisms: "Whoever fights monsters should see to it that in the process he does not become a monster. And when you look long into an abyss, the abyss also looks into you" (*Beyond Good and Evil*, 146).

8 "there is a necessary vice": The typescripts read "there is a necessity to sin."

8 "For the garden is the only place there is": This section is an exercise in *apophasis*, or "negative theology," and as such is highly reminiscent of some of T. S. Eliot's poems in that spirit, especially "Ash-Wednesday"—"Where shall the word be found, where will the word / Resound? Not here"—and "East Coker":

> I said to my soul, be still, and wait without hope
> For hope would be hope for the wrong thing; wait without love
> For love would be love of the wrong thing; there is yet faith
> But the faith and love and the hope are all in the waiting.
> Wait without thought, for you are not ready for thought:
> So the darkness shall be the light, and the stillness the dancing.

9 "that immortal and nameless Centre": This seems to be a reference to the statement—attributed to everyone from Empedocles to Voltaire—that "God is a circle whose center is everywhere and circumference nowhere." It first appears in a twelfth-century text where it is attributed to the legendary Hermes Trismegistus. Auden may have encountered it in Nietzsche's exposition of the doctrine of eternal recurrence in the third part of *Thus Spoke Zarathustra*. For the history of the phrase, see Robin Small, "Nietzsche and a Platonist Tradition of the Cosmos: Center Everywhere and Circumference Nowhere," *Journal of the History of Ideas* 44:1 (January–March 1983): 89–104.

9 "the turbine of time": When in early 1943 Auden taught a course at Swarthmore College called Romanticism from Rousseau to Hitler, he prepared a chart for his students (see *LA* 240) that outlines the previous two centuries' intellectual history as a series of varying positions taken with reference to a set of categories. In relation to "Time" he contrasts the image of time as a circle ("Natural, Cyclical, Reversible") with the image of time as a turbine ("Static, Eternal, Unchanging"). Both of these he treats as errors: the orthodox view of time, according to the chart, is best represented by a spiral ("Historical, Irreversible, Process Change").

9 "O would I could mourn over Fate": A recurrent and central theme in Auden's work is the distinction between human beings, who live in History

and must make choices, and all other creatures, who obey the dictates of Nature because they cannot do otherwise. In "Homage to Clio" he writes of "birds who chirp, / Not for effect but because chirping / Is the thing to do" (*CP* 608); conversely, he writes in the eighteenth of his "Sonnets from China," "We live in freedom by necessity" (*CP* 192)—the one choice humans cannot make is that of escaping from choice.

10 "The Annunciation": Here Auden's poem takes up the biblical narrative, at the point in the Gospel of Luke (1:26–38) when the angel Gabriel announces to Mary that, though a virgin, she will give birth to the Messiah of Israel.

10 "The Four Faculties": In his *Integration of the Personality*, trans. Stanley Dell (New York: Farrar and Rinehart, 1939), Jung writes, "Four is also the number of the basic psychological functions: sensation, thinking, feeling, intuition. It is only at a relatively advanced stage of consciousness that the four functions are separated and given specific valuation" (38). See also the Introduction, page xxiv. Each of the Faculties here reports on a vision, and each vision is of an allegorical landscape, after the fashion of the *paysage moralisé* tradition, of which Auden was fond and about which he wrote an early poem ("Paysage Moralisé," *CP* 119). The fullest development of this kind of conceit comes in "The Seven Stages," the third part of Auden's longest poem, *The Age of Anxiety*: in that part the poem's four characters, highly developed and particularized versions of the Four Faculties, travel through their own allegorical landscape, which each of them perceives in dramatically different ways (*CP* 483–512).

12 "Putti of Venus": *Putti* are representations of small children, usually boys with wings, in Italian Renaissance and baroque art. Cupid (son of Venus) is often so represented.

12 "that hidden / Garden": At the conclusion of the narrative of the Fall, Adam and Eve are expelled from the Garden of Eden: "So he drove out the man; and he placed at the east of the garden of Eden Cherubims, and a flaming sword which turned every way, to keep the way of the tree of life" (Genesis 3:34).

13 "one boisterous preposter": Auden seems to have coined "preposter" as a nominative form of the adjective "preposterous." The word does not to my knowledge appear elsewhere.

15 "None may wake there": Mary is the one who may wake in the garden, because she will give birth to the Child, Jesus, whose task is to restore hu-

manity to the state of perfect obedience to and fellowship with God that
were lost in Adam's "act of / Rebellion."

16 "When Eve, in love": In Christian theology Mary is often said to be the
"second Eve," undoing through her obedience—"Behold the handmaiden
of the Lord" (Luke 1:38)—what Eve had done through her disobedience.
Thus Gabriel says, "What her negation wounded, may / Your affirmation
heal to-day."

16 "Since Adam, being free to choose": Auden begins his poem "Friday's
Child" (*CP* 673) with these stanzas:

> He told us we were free to choose
> But, children as we were, we thought—
> "Paternal Love will only use
> Force in the last resort
>
> On those too bumptious to repent."
> Accustomed to religious dread,
> It never crossed our minds He meant
> Exactly what He said.

16 "The shadow of his images": A Platonic metaphor. In the *Republic*, bk. 7,
people chained in a cave watch shadows of things projected on the cave's
walls, and are unable to see the things themselves. They are turned away
from what is real. Similarly, in "Terce," the second of Auden's "*Horae Ca-
nonicae*," he writes, "now each of us / Prays to an image of his image of
himself" (*CP* 627).

18 "The Demolisher arrives": Death.

18 "The Temptation of St. Joseph": On Joseph as an autobiographical charac-
ter, see the Introduction, page xxvi.

19 "*Joseph, you have heard*": The typescripts have, in place of this passage, these
lines:

> *Joseph the Just was sober and staid,*
> *He chiselled a living from the carpentry trade;*
> *Mary his love, was alone a lot;*
> *That leads to trouble, believe it or not.*

19 "*Mary may be pure*": The typescripts have, in place of this passage, these lines:

> *Joseph the Worker sweated away*
> *With hammer and plane through the heat of the day.*

> *Mary, his sweetheart, sat in the wood,*
> *Catching a chill that changed her for good.*

20 *"Maybe, maybe not"*: The typescripts have, in place of this passage, these lines:

> *Mary the Modest was met in the lane*
> *By Someone or Something she couldn't explain.*
> *Joseph the Honest looked up and God's eye*
> *Was winking at him through a hole in the sky.*

At this point the typescripts add another stanza:

> Disjointed items stopped my life to say
> How proud they were to satisfy
>   My own true love:
> Hair, muscle, clothing noses, necks,
> A prince's purse, a sailor's sex
>   Appeal;
> And my horns grew up to the sky;
> When I asked if they were real,
> All giggled and ran away.

For the biographical context of these lines, see the Introduction, p. xxvi. In the typescripts the stanza is followed by one more italicized quatrain:

> *Mary the Maiden, merry and mild*
> *Walked down to the brook and came back with a child.*
> *Joseph the Gentle is a jilted Jew.*
> *Where's the wild father? The fun is on you.*

Then follows the section beginning "Where are you, Father, where?"

21 "Be silent, and sit still": The emphasis on silence and stillness once again recalls Eliot's "Four Quartets," but also Pascal's dictum "I have often said that the sole cause of man's unhappiness is that he does not know how to stay quietly in his room" (*Pensées*, 136).

21 "For the perpetual excuse": In Genesis 3:11–12, when God confronts Adam—"Hast thou eaten of the tree, whereof I commanded thee that thou shouldest not eat?"—Adam replies, "The woman whom thou gavest to be with me, she gave me of the tree, and I did eat."

22 "For likening Love to war": That is, for thinking of sexual relations in terms of conquests, after the fashion of Don Juan. For Auden the Don Juan

archetype was a central one: see his essay "Don Juan" in *The Dyer's Hand*, which, significantly, he placed in the section of the book particularly devoted to the relations between Christianity and art (*P4* 735–41).

22 "a non-essential luxury": True in this case because Mary will bear a child without having had sex; but the scientifically literate Auden would have known that many animals reproduce by parthenogenesis ("virgin birth"), in which the male plays no part.

23 "You both must act": The typescripts read "You both must love."

24 "The Green Bohemia of that myth": The myth that it is possible to return to the Garden, that is, to innocence, by one's own efforts. "Bohemia" here certainly refers to "Bohemian-ism"—a "romantic" and artistic (or pseudo-artistic) rejection of social conventions and mores in favor of a freer authenticity of being—but also perhaps to one of the greenest of Shakespeare's "green worlds," the Bohemia of *The Winter's Tale*.

24 "Simultaneous passions make": A reference to Tristan and Isolde, whose story Auden believed to be the paradigmatic myth of erotic love.

24 "Independent embryos": Even the division and multiplication of cells by mitosis embodies rebellion, the urge for independence and separation.

26 "The Summons": First the "wise men from the east" (Matthew 2:1) are summoned, and then those who are ordered to register for taxation: "And it came to pass in those days, that there went out a decree from Caesar Augustus, that all the world should be taxed. (And this taxing was first made when Cyrenius was governor of Syria.) And all went to be taxed, every one into his own city. And Joseph also went up from Galilee, out of the city of Nazareth, into Judaea, unto the city of David, which is called Bethlehem; (because he was of the house and lineage of David:) To be taxed with Mary his espoused wife, being great with child" (Luke 2:1–5).

26 "sophrosyne": Moderation, temperance, or, as the Oracle of Delphi was traditionally said to put it, "Nothing too much." Words of the same root appear occasionally in the New Testament, as when St. Paul writes, "For I say, through the grace given unto me, to every man that is among you, not to think of himself more highly than he ought to think; but to think soberly [*sophronein*], according as God hath dealt to every man the measure of faith."

26 "Glassy Mountain": It is possible, as John Fuller suggests (*JF* 350), that this refers to one of the Grimms' tales, "The Seven Ravens," in which a girl tries to rescue her brothers, who have all turned into ravens, and are imprisoned in the otherwise undescribed Glassy Mountain. But the context may only

suggest a surface on which one can get no grip, a metaphor for insoluble intellectual problems.

26 "that Bridge of Dread": John Fuller points out that a "Brig o' Dread" leads to Purgatory in the anonymous fifteenth-century ballad "A Lyke-Wake Dirge" (*JF* 350).

27 "To break down Her defenses": In both typescripts, Auden follows the speech of each Wise Man, and then their collective speech, with a limerick. In T2 these are crossed through and a note is added in Auden's hand at the end of the typescript: "Limericks all cut." Since so many traditional limericks begin "There was an old man," that genre offers a way of gently, or not so gently, mocking the pretensions of the agèd to wisdom. The one that succeeds the First (scientifically-minded) Wise Man is:

> *There was an Old Man of Cathay*
> *Who would peep after lunch every day*
> *Through a chink in the wall*
> *At nothing at all*
> *And walk very quickly away.*

In his "Notes on the Comic" that Auden would include in *The Dyer's Hand* he comments on the logic of comic rhymes, using as his prime example a limerick beginning "There was an Old Man of Whitehaven" (*P4* 721).

27 "A thorough inquisition": In his *Instauratio Magna* (1620) Francis Bacon writes of his "law-like, chaste, and severe inquisition" of nature—what is commonly called "putting nature to the question." In his essay on *Othello*, "The Joker in the Pack" (written probably in 1960), Auden would claim that "Iago's treatment of Othello conforms to Bacon's definition of scientific enquiry as putting nature to the Question" (*P4* 643).

27 "My faith that in Time's constant": The limerick that, in the typescripts, follows this stanza is clearly meant to satirize Yeats (whose late poem "Under Ben Bulben" concludes with the epitaph he wrote for himself: "Cast a cold eye / On life, on death. / Horseman, pass by!"):

> *There was an Old Man who would stamp*
> *Whenever the weather got damp,*
> *Shouting—"Cast a cold eye*
> *Upon Death." They said—"Why?*
> *My dear, at your age it's a camp."*

27 "Observing how myopic": The limerick that, in the typescripts, follows this
stanza is this:

> *There was an old man of Balbec*
> *Who kept his emotions in check*
> > *By taking cold showers*
> > *And smelling wild flowers.*
> *They called him That-Pain-in-the-Neck.*

Some of Proust's *À la recherche du temps perdu* is set in the fictional town of
Balbec.

27 "Venus of the Soma": "Soma" is Greek for "body," thus indicating a purely
physical erotic desire.

28 "The weather has been awful": A strong echo of T. S. Eliot's 1930 poem
"Journey of the Magi," which opens with these lines:

> A cold coming we had of it,
> Just the worst time of the year
> For a journey, and such a long journey:
> The ways deep and the weather sharp,
> The very dead of winter.

Eliot, in turn, was quoting with slight emendation a sermon that Lancelot
Andrewes preached before King James at Whitehall on Christmas Day of
1622: "Last we consider the time of their coming, the season of the year.
It was no summer progress. A cold coming they had of it at this time of the
year, just the worst time of the year to take a journey, and specially a long
journey. The ways deep, the weather sharp, the days short, the sun farthest
off, *in solsitio brumali,* 'the very dead of winter.'"

The limerick that, in the typescripts, succeeds this stanza is this:

> *There were Three Old Men travelled miles*
> *In search of the Fortunate Isles,*
> > *Till they cried—"It's a shame;*
> > *All hotels are the same,*
> *And we suffer acutely from piles."*

The Fortunate Isles, or the Isles of the Blessed, are in Greek mythology a
place of endless bliss, reserved for the souls of mortals particularly favored
by the gods.

28 "fosse": A ditch.

30 "Great is Caesar": In the margin of a page in the Berg notebook Auden
jots down his meanings for Caesar's seven kingdoms, though not in order:

1	Abstraction
2	Natural Cause
3	Number
6	Drugs
5	Power
7	Propaganda
4	Money

30 "S's with P's": Subjects with Predicates, according to the notation of sym-
bolic logic.

30 "Harsh is the Law": From Giambattista Vico's *Scienza Nuova* (1725),
111.322: "*Lex dura est, sed certa est.*"

31 "The Transcendentals": Transcendental numbers, like π, are nonalgebraic
real numbers; as the mathematician Leonhard Euler wrote, they "tran-
scend the power of algebraic methods." The comma separating "a few inte-
gers" from "the Transcendentals" was added by Auden to the proofs of the
1968 *Collected Longer Poems*.

31 "Whee-Spree": In a letter to Theodore Spencer (29 April 1943), Auden
wrote, "'Whee-spree' was supplied me by an American for everything-goes
absurdity. If anyone can give me a better term with the same meaning, and
the same linguistic structure, I should be grateful, as it doesn't sound quite
right to me" (HUA).

31 "When the Barbarian invades": Here especially, but also later in the cho-
rus, are echoes of 1 Esdras 4 (an addition to or variation on the biblical
book of Ezra): "But yet the king is more mighty: for he is lord of all these
things, and hath dominion over them; and whatsoever he commandeth
them they do. If he bid them make war the one against the other, they do
it: if he send them out against the enemies, they go, and break down moun-
tains walls and towers" (verses 3–4). In light of the chorus's refrain, "Great
is Caesar," it is noteworthy that later in the chapter the king says, "Blessed
be the God of truth," after which "all the people then shouted, and said,
Great is Truth, and mighty above all things" (verses 40–41).

32 "History is in the making": In the typescripts this line is introduced by quota-
tion marks, and the quotation is closed with the words "a thousand years."

32 "free-thinking Jews": Auden's admiration for T. S. Eliot is often clear in
this poem, but here is a moment of sharp critique: in the most notorious

passage in *After Strange Gods: A Primer of Modern Heresy* (New York: Harcourt, Brace and Company, 1934), a book he suppressed soon after writing it, Eliot commented that "unity of religious background" is essential to a healthy society, and therefore "reasons of race and religion combine to make any large number of free-thinking Jews undesirable."

33 "For Powers and Times": The typescripts read "Power and Time."

33 "Our Father, whose": An adaptation of the Lord's Prayer. Auden got from William Blake the idea that people who utter the prescribed words may in actuality be praying something tailored to their needs and preferences. He concluded his review of Cochrane's *Christianity and Classical Culture* by quoting Blake's bitterly satirical revision of the Lord's Prayer, which begins thus: "Our Father Augustus Caesar who art in these thy Substantial Astronomical Telescopic Heavens, Holiness to Thy Name or Title, and reverence to Thy Shadow" (from his 1827 annotations to a "New Translation of the Lord's Prayer" by Dr. Thornton, in *The Complete Poetry & Prose of William Blake*, rev. ed., ed. David V. Erdman [New York: Anchor Books, 1988], 669).

Apparently Theodore Spencer, to whom Auden had sent a late draft of the poem, objected to the line-ending prepositions in this section. Auden responded in a letter of 29 April 1943, "The prepositions in the Chorale. This was intentional stressing. Partly because I like the Scotch metrical psalms which do it" (HUA). That version of the Psalter was approved by the Church of Scotland in 1650. As an illustration of what Auden had in mind, here is the first stanza of Psalm 51:

> After thy loving-kindness, Lord,
>   have mercy upon me:
> For thy compassions great, blot out
>   all mine iniquity.

34 "A smudged and crooked line": Paul Claudel, whom Auden refers to in his 1939 poem "In Memory of W. B. Yeats," wrote a verse drama called *Le soulier de satin* (The satin slipper) that he prefaced with what he called a "Portuguese proverb": "*Deus escreve direito por linas tortas*," or "God writes straight with crooked lines."

34 "Adventure, Art, and Peace": In *Adventures of Ideas* (New York: Simon and Schuster, 1933), Alfred North Whitehead claims that "the five qualities" are "Truth, Beauty, Adventure, Art, Peace." In 1963, in a copy of his 1945 *Collected Poetry* owned by a Yale undergraduate named Robert Franklin, Auden

wrote next to this chorale, "pure Whitehead; put in out of respect for 'music' to follow spoken."

34 "The Vision of the Shepherds": See Luke 2:8–20. For the role of the Shepherds, see the Introduction, page xxxi. In the typescripts the speakers in this first section are indicated only in the page margin, thus revealing the section more clearly as a single poem with no stanza divisions.

In the typescripts this section (concluding with "we shall hear the Good News") is followed by a poem—written in an Americanized idiom similar to that used in *Paul Bunyan*—which Britten would later set under the title "Shepherds' Carol":

> *O lift your little pinkie*
> *And touch the winter sky:*
> *Love is all over the mountains*
> *Where the beautiful go to die.*
>
> If Time were the wicked sheriff,
>   In a horse opera,
> I'd pay for riding lessons
>   And take his gun away.
>
> If I were a Valentino,
>   And Fortune were a broad,
> I'd hypnotise that iceberg
>   Till she kissed me of her own accord.
>
> If I'd stacked up the velvet
>   And my crooked rib were dead,
> I'd be breeding white canaries
>   And eating crackers in bed.
>
> But my cuffs are soiled and fraying.
>   The kitchen clock is slow,
> And over the Blue Waters
>   The grass grew long ago.
>
> I ain't speaking through the flowers
>   Nor trying to explain,
> But there ain't a living sorrow
>   Comes wrapped in cellophane.

O solid is the sending
  Of the Boogie Woogie Man;
But who has found the horseshoes
  Or danced on Fiddler's Green?

O lift your little pinkie
  And touch the winter sky:
Love is all over the mountains
  Where the beautiful go to die.

In T2 a line runs through this poem, and a note at the end of the typescript—in Auden's hand, clearly directed to Britten—reads "The lyric O lift your little pinkie is cut. Substitute for it the following. (Maybe in sentimental jazz style?)" He then writes out the lyric "Levers ask the aching wrist," just as it would appear in the published version, though there he would substitute "nudge" for "ask." Apparently Theodore Spencer, to whom Auden had sent a draft of the poem, disliked this lyric, for in April of 1943 Auden wrote to him, "Am afraid you're probably right about the shepherds song. Something, I feel, is needed, and with a certain 'City' flavor.... Must I re-do it completely?" (HUA).

Britten's setting of "O lift your little pinkie" uses the first stanza as a chorus, repeating it after each of the other stanzas; he also omits the stanzas beginning "I ain't speaking through the flowers" and "O solid is the sending."

37 "Unto you a Child": Cf. Isaiah 9:6: "For unto us a child is born, unto us a son is given: and the government shall be upon his shoulder: and his name shall be called Wonderful, Counsellor, the mighty God, the everlasting Father, the Prince of Peace." In the typescripts "Child" and "Son" are not capitalized. In the Berg notebook drafts of this passage are much longer than the final version: one comprises three nineteen-line stanzas.

38 "Sing Glory to God": Cf. the song of the angels to the shepherds, "Glory to God in the highest, and on earth peace, good will toward men" (Luke 2:14).

39 "The children of men": A phrase often used to describe humanity in the Hebrew Bible, especially the Psalms. Among the more relevant here may be Psalm 14:2, "The Lord looked down from heaven upon the children of men, to see if there were any that did understand, and seek God," and Psalm 36:7, "How excellent is thy lovingkindness, O God! therefore the children of men put their trust under the shadow of thy wings."

40 "At the Manger": This poem was first printed in *Commonweal*, 25 December 1942. In "Hic et Ille," one of the sets of notes and aphorisms included in *The Dyer's Hand*, Auden writes, "A task for an existentialist theologian: to preach a sermon on the topic *The Sleep of Christ*" (*P4* 525).

40 "the Sorrowful Way": The *Via Dolorosa*, the path Jesus followed as he carried his cross through Jerusalem to Golgotha, the place of execution. In 1939 Auden had written a poem called "Blessed Event" (*CP* 302) that treats the Nativity obliquely by describing the nature of "any blessed event"; it ends thus:

> And the New Life awkwardly touches its home, beginning to fumble
> About in the Truth for the straight successful Way
> Which will always appear to end in some dreadful defeat.

40 "First Wise Man": In Robert Franklin's copy of the 1945 *Collected Poetry*, Auden wrote next to this section, "numerology is pagan."

43 "Our weakness": The idea that "weakness" and ineptitude can be vehicles of grace is a major theme in much of Auden's poetry in the 1940s, especially "The Sea and the Mirror," whose longest section, "Caliban to the Audience," concludes with a vision of spectacular artistic failure that paradoxically opens the way to devotion: in failure "we are blessed by that Wholly Other Life ... it is just here, among the ruins and the bones, that we may rejoice in the perfected Work which is not ours" (*CP* 442). In his 1949 poem "Memorial for the City," Auden would associate "Our weakness" with the human body (*CP* 593).

44 "our tall errors of imagination": Cf. Trinculo's song in Auden's next long poem, "The Sea and the Mirror" (*CP* 421), in which artistic imagination (elevating and isolating) is also figured as tallness:

> Mechanic, merchant, king,
> Are warmed by the cold clown
> Whose head is in the clouds
> And never can get down....
>
> Wild images, come down
> Out of your freezing sky,
> That I, like shorter men,
> May get my joke and die.

46 "The choice to love is open till we die": Cf. the line from "September 1, 1939" that Auden later renounced, "We must love one another or die" (*SP* 97).

47 "once known complete intimacy": An intimacy exemplified in Adam's task of naming the creatures: "And out of the ground the LORD God formed every beast of the field, and every fowl of the air; and brought them unto Adam to see what he would call them: and whatsoever Adam called every living creature, that was the name thereof" (Genesis 2:19). Auden would have been aware of the long-standing Christian tradition that Adam, with exact and immediate intuition, chose names that matched the very being of the creature named.

47 "moods of the rose": This is the reading in all editions except *Collected Longer Poems* (1968), in which the phrase reads, "the moods and the ambitions of the swallow." The 1968 text resulted from Auden's mistaken correction of a printer's error. The compositor omitted "the rose or," leaving "the moods of the ambitions of the swallow"; Auden, having forgotten what he originally wrote, simply altered the first "of" to "and." The correct reading was restored posthumously in the 1976 *Collected Poems*.

48 "could be unlocked": In correcting proof for *Collected Longer Poems* (1968), Auden changed "would" (the reading in *For the Time Being* and *The Collected Poetry*) to "could."

48 "the emancipation of Time from Space": Possibly a reference to Einstein's theory of special relativity, which was generally understood to make the passage of time relative to motion.

48 "the Revolution of the Images": Probably a reference to Freudian psychoanalysis, in which repressed and then recovered memories "rise up" and alter the analysand's self-understanding, "cast[ing] into subjection the senses by Whom hitherto they had been enslaved."

49 "Original Sin": From Augustine's phrase *peccatum originalis*, the condition of being born into sin which—as Augustine believed, drawing on Paul's letter to the Romans—afflicts all human beings since the Fall.

49 "Tree of Knowledge": See Genesis 2:9, "And out of the ground made the LORD God to grow every tree that is pleasant to the sight, and good for food; the tree of life also in the midst of the garden, and the tree of knowledge of good and evil."

49 "*The bravest drew back*": In the typescripts drafts this line reads, "The brave knew better than to say Boo to the Abyss."

49 "From the beginning until now": See Hebrews 1:1–2, "God, who at sundry times and in divers manners spake in time past unto the fathers by the prophets, hath in these last days spoken unto us by his Son."

49 "the Word should be made Flesh": Cf. John 1:14, "And the Word was made flesh, and dwelt among us, (and we beheld his glory, the glory as of the only begotten of the Father,) full of grace and truth." Auden was always aware that the Pauline term "flesh" (Greek *sarx*) is bound to be misunderstood. In his essay "Balaam and His Ass" he would write, "It is unfortunate that the word 'Flesh,' set in contrast to 'Spirit,' is bound to suggest not what the Gospels and St Paul intended it to mean, the whole physical-historical nature of fallen man, but his physical nature alone, a suggestion very welcome to our passion for reproving and improving others instead of examining our own consciences" (*P4* 545–46).

50 "in the Beginning and in the End": Cf. Revelation 1:8, "I am Alpha and Omega, the beginning and the ending, saith the Lord"; also Revelation 1:11, 21:6, 22:13.

50 "I AM": Cf. Exodus 3:13–14, where Yahweh tells Moses that his name is "I AM." In traditional Christian theology Jesus is thought to affirm his identity with this God when, in debate with Jewish leaders, he says, "Your father Abraham rejoiced to see my day: and he saw it, and was glad. Then said the Jews unto him, Thou art not yet fifty years old, and hast thou seen Abraham? Jesus said unto them, Verily, verily, I say unto you, Before Abraham was, I am" (John 8:56–58).

In coupling the "I AM" with "THOU ART," Auden draws on the Jewish theologian Martin Buber's *Ich und Du* (1923), translated into English by Ronald Gregor Smith as *I and Thou* (New York: Charles Scribner's Sons, 1937).

In *For the Time Being* (1944) this reads "THOU ART"; Auden changed it to "HE IS" for *The Collected Poetry* (1945).

50 "we are bold to say": In the service of Holy Communion in the *Book of Common Prayer* the Lord's Prayer is introduced by these words from the priest: "And now, as our Saviour Christ hath taught us, we are bold to say...."

50 "He is in no sense a symbol": See the Introduction, page xxxiv.

51 "all men love themselves": In the typescripts this reads, "man loves himself."

51 "each man loves God": When Jesus is asked, "which is the great commandment in the law?" he replies, "Thou shalt love the Lord thy God with all thy

heart, and with all thy soul, and with all thy mind. This is the first and great commandment. And the second is like unto it, Thou shalt love thy neighbour as thyself. On these two commandments hang all the law and the prophets" (Matthew 22:36–40).

51 "promiscuous fornication": Cochrane, *Christianity and Classical Culture*, 418: "For such perversions of intellectual activity Augustine has a name and it is a strong one: he calls them *fantastica fornicatio*, the prostitution of the mind to its own fancies. To him, therefore, they represented, in its grossest and ugliest aspect, the betrayal of understanding. As such, they were errors of the scientific intelligence in its effort to become an instrument of control. That is to say, they originated from the temptation to eat of the tree of knowledge rather than of the tree of life." Augustine uses this phrase in *De Trinitate* (On the Trinity), 12.9.14.

51 "Roland": From the medieval French epic *The Song of Roland*, which centers on a small group of Frankish knights overwhelmed by a vast army of Saracens. Brünnhilde is a Valkyrie in Norse mythology and a major figure in Wagner's *Ring* cycle. Simeon's argument that the Incarnation makes possible a total revaluation of heroism and excellence is restated a little later by Herod, but for Herod this revaluation is precisely why the Child cannot be allowed to live.

51 "the woodcutter's simple-minded son": This and "the washerwoman's butter-fingered daughter" are representative figures from folktales in which the humble are raised to the heights.

52 "a logical In-Order-That": In his essay "On the Difference between a Genius and an Apostle" Kierkegaard wrote, "No genius has an *in order that*: the Apostle has absolutely and paradoxically an *in order that*." Auden would have known this in Alexander Dru's translation, *The Present Age and Two Minor Ethico-Religious Treatises* (London: Oxford University Press, 1940). Auden would later write his own essay called "Genius & Apostle" (*P4* 759–75) and use the Kierkegaard quotation above as its epigraph.

52 "the Barbarians, deny the Unity": Simeon is here defending Trinitarian theology as being neither simple monotheism nor simply polytheism; God is, rather, "Three-in-One." His language here evokes a section of the Athanasian Creed: "And the catholic faith is this: That we worship one God in Trinity, and Trinity in Unity; Neither confounding the persons nor dividing the substance."

52 "co-inherence": On this concept developed by Charles Williams, see the
    Introduction, page xiv. The hyphen was mistakenly dropped from the 1991
    and 2007 reset editions of the posthumous *Collected Poems* (first published
    1976) because it occurred at the end of a line of type in the 1976 edition.
    The hyphen is present in all texts printed in Auden's lifetime.

52 "*Our lost Appearances*": In ancient and medieval cosmology, "saving the ap-
    pearances" is explaining the motions of the heavenly bodies in a way that
    accounts, as fully as possible, for what they are seen to do. Thus in the Ptol-
    emaic system epicycles were posited to account for apparent retrograde
    motion. In his 1958 poem "Friday's Child" (*CP*674–75) Auden would write,

> Meanwhile, a silence on the Cross,
> As dead as we shall ever be,
> Speaks of some total gain or loss,
>   And you and I are free
>
> To guess from the insulted face
> Just what Appearances He saves
> By suffering in a public place
>   A death reserved for slaves.

And the Berg notebook contains a draft of a passage, apparently to be
spoken by some voice of temptation serving a similar function to the voice
in "Levers nudge the aching wrist," that reads thus:

> What has occurred that could deserve your love?
> The Real is what Time makes it, facile stuff,
> [Like] Number, acquiescent and [depraved].
> O [famished] lover, rise, and come to me,
> The radiant queen of Possibility,
> By whom the lost Appearances are saved,
> With whom alone it can be time to die.

53 "The Massacre of the Innocents": The second chapter of Matthew's Gos-
    pel is occupied with a story about what happened when Herod the Great,
    the king of Judea by allowance of the Romans, learned that "the King of the
    Jews" had been born and wanted to destroy this rival. Not knowing who the
    child is, Herod "was exceeding wroth, and sent forth, and slew all the chil-

dren that were in Bethlehem, and in all the coasts thereof, from two years old and under." In Robert Franklin's copy of the 1945 *Collected Poetry*, Auden wrote, "I'm sure there's a bit of Herod in me."

53 "Because I am bewildered": Herod's speech here parodies the *Meditations* of the philosopher and (from 161 to 180 CE) Roman emperor Marcus Aurelius, which begins with similar expressions of gratitude: "From my grandfather Verus I learned good morals and the government of my temper. From the reputation and remembrance of my father, modesty and a manly character." And so on.

In the Berg notebook there are a number of pages containing what appear to be drafts of Herod's speech in verse form. Several versions of the speech begin with these lines:

> Our first adolescent efforts are scarcely more
> Than a substitute for the nursery rocking horse
> On which we rode away from a father's imperfect justice ...

Lines very similar to these would be given to Prospero in "The Sea and the Mirror": see *CP* 405.

Herod's monologue was first printed in *Harper's Magazine*, December 1943, under the title "Herod Considers the Massacre of the Innocents." The text is identical to the one printed here except for minor variations in spelling and the absence of some commas found in the final text.

53 "Tetrarch": Herod the Great was not in fact tetrarch, but king. After his death the Romans divided the Kingdom of Judea and gave Herod's sons rulership over the parts, thus forming the Tetrarchy.

54 "Brown on Resolution": The title of a 1929 adventure novel by C. S. Forester, but Auden's joke is that the title can be read as that of a stoic tract about resolution by someone named Brown.

54 "Achilles and the Tortoise": Otherwise known as Zeno's paradox against motion. Since swift-footed Achilles, who has given the tortoise a hefty head start in a footrace, must cover half the distance separating them before he can overtake the tortoise, and then half the remainder, and then half that, ad infinitum, it is clear that he can never in fact overtake the tortoise.

55 "faubourgs": Suburbs; used in Paris to refer to parts of the city that were formerly suburban.

55 "turn tables or feel bumps": "Table-turning" or "table-tipping" is a form of séance in which letters of the alphabet are called out: when the table turns

or tips at the call of a letter, that letter is written down, and eventually messages are spelled out. Phrenology was a nineteenth-century pseudoscience that claimed that character could be read through the pattern and placement of bumps on people's skulls.

56 "begot a hero": The idea that society can be rescued by a hero-king is, Cochrane argues, central to the classical ideal: see the Introduction, page xvii. Such belief has its modern counterpart in, for instance, the Nazi cult of the Führer. Auden explores and critiques this idea most fully in the fourth part of *The Age of Anxiety*, "The Dirge," a lament for "Our lost dad, / Our colossal father" (*CP* 513).

56 "an ecstatic grin": The typescripts read "a silly ecstasy."

58 "When the Sex War ended": About this section Auden wrote to Theodore Spencer on 29 April 1943 (HUA): "The particular horror effect I am aiming for is that, to the soldier, killing is a professional job, about which he doesn't think. George is, of course, the Archetype of the soldier. Musically, Britten and I thought that maybe he should set it for young girls' voices (the ugliest sound on earth) very high up with piccolos, triangles etc." In Robert Franklin's copy of the 1945 *Collected Poetry*, Auden wrote next to this section, "Homosexual."

60 "The Flight into Egypt": This section provides another example of Auden's fondness for the allegorized landscape, the *paysage moralisé*: see Introduction, page xxxv, and the note concerning the "Four Faculties," page 75.

About this section, and how it related to the Narrator's concluding monologue, Auden made some important comments to Theodore Spencer in his letter of 29 April 1943 (HUA): "The Egypt-Christmas tree transition. The madness does not belong to Egypt but to the desert on the way there (a parallel to the Temptation in the Wilderness). The light may shine in darkness but to us, it's [*sic*] life is hid, because we have sent it away, ie the immediate Post-Christmas temptation is that of the emotional let-down of an intense experience which is then suddenly over. I tried to introduce the sweeter note in the last section. ie if the light is to be seen again, it is by going forward (to the Passion perhaps) and not by nostalgic reminiscence. One cannot be a little child; one has to become like one, and to do that one has to leave home, to lose even what seems now most good."

61 "The silly he locked": The first impression of the U.S. first edition of *For the Time Being* (1944), followed by the British edition of 1945, has "looked"; Auden corrected the error in the second impression of the U.S. edition, and the corrected version appears in all later texts.

63 "Fly, Holy Family": At the end of T2 Auden writes this lyric out by hand with instructions that it should be inserted just before the Narrator's concluding monologue. It was not present in earlier drafts.

63 "Well, so that is that": First printed in *Harper's Magazine*, January 1944, under the title "After Christmas: A Passage from a Christmas Oratorio." It is identical to the version printed here except for minor variations in spelling, the absence of some commas found in the final text, and paragraph breaks before "The Christmas Feast" and "They will come."

65 "the Time Being to redeem": See Ephesians 5:15–16, "See then that ye walk circumspectly, not as fools, but as wise, Redeeming the time, because the days are evil."

65 "The night of agony": A reference to the Agony in the Garden, Jesus's time of fearful prayer in the Garden of Gethsemane (Matthew 26:36–46); also evoked here is Psalm 91:6, which speaks of "the demon that wasteth at noonday." At least since the fourth-century ascetic Evagrius of Pontus, the "noonday demon" has been associated with acedia and melancholy. Melancholy is perhaps the essential symptom of psycho-spiritual anxiety, thus the instruction a few lines farther along to "Seek Him in the Kingdom of Anxiety."

65 "God will cheat no one": Cf. Kafka's aphorism, "One must not cheat anybody, not even the world of its triumph" (*The Great Wall of China: Stories and Reflections*, trans. Willa and Edwin Muir [London: M. Secker, 1933], 172). In the typescripts the two lines of the speech read,

> That God's will be done, that, (to paraphrase Kafka,)
> "God will cheat no one, not even the world of its triumph."

But in the handwritten appendix to T2 Auden gives instructions to edit the penultimate line. He does not mention deletion of the quotation marks in the final line, so it is not clear when they were cut.

65 "He is the Way": See John 14:6, "Jesus saith unto him, I am the way, the truth, and the life: no man cometh unto the Father, but by me."

65 "the land of Unlikeness": Probably from Augustine's *Confessions*, bk. 7. In Pusey's translation, which Auden would have known: "I found myself to be a long way from thee in the region of unlikeness [*in regione dissimilitudinis*]" (JF 355). But the exact phrase "land of unlikeness" appears frequently in Etienne Gilson's *The Mystical Theology of St. Bernard* (New York: Sheed and Ward, 1940), and one chapter of the book is titled *"Regione Dissimilitudinis."*

65 "the World of the Flesh": On Auden's view of the proper Christian meaning of "Flesh," see note above, page 87.